My Way!

Finding My Way Back to Me

DE'BROADA CORNELIUS

iCreativBooks

Kansas

iCreativ Books

an imprint of iCreativ Properti, LLC.
6505 E. Central Suite #314,
Wichita KS 67206

First Printing: March 2017

My Way! Finding My Way Back to Me
Copyright ©2016 by De'Broada L. Cornelius

Printed in the United States of America.

My Way! Finding My Way Back to Me.
ISBN: 978-0-692-81365-2

iCreativ Publishing
6505 E. Central Suite #314,
Wichita KS 67206
www.icreativproperti.com

My Way!

Finding My Way Back to Me

For Cameron, Erica and Khristah

You will fall down
You will hurt
But don't ever give up
Never, ever give up on yourself

CONTENTS

TWO

WORK THROUGH YOUR STUFF! (Get Out of Your Way)

THREE
CHANGE YOUR MINDSET (MAKE ROOM FOR YOU)

Introduction

Why write an introduction while feeling frustrated? Well, I have to start some place and I prefer to put the energy into what I'm passionate about.

I find myself saying, "I'm so annoyed, what am I going to do?" Anxiety swells my chest causing my stomach to tighten and deepen the sigh of my frustration. I'm so sick of feeling this way. I'm sick of getting upset about things beyond my control or, snide comments made by those unaware of what I'm thinking. Then I think, "I really don't like people." Hold up...that's not true. Okay, let me think about that. No, it's not true. I plug my ears and quiet myself.

Listening within, it's not that I don't like people. I simply enjoy time alone and limit the sharing of my passion to like-minded people and avoid the energy of criticism, as much as possible. That's normal, right? Anyway, who cares? I'm working on me. Reality is, we see others according to our own perception or, filter which is usually quite different than the actual person.

Being so, I am a writer, a lover of words— written words. Due to a lack of devotion and nurturing of my craft, I created a state of inner turmoil (anxiety) which manifested through procrastination and frustration. For years, I felt stuck. Indecisively, I went back and forth and successfully prevented the accomplishment of putting my thoughts on paper and my point of view in book format. All the while knowing I have something good to share.

Writing and connecting with people is my gift. I know it because I love it and the fulfillment I receive when I allow myself to just be "me." Even more, many confide and share desires, dreams and fears with me and are so appreciative of the guidance I've given. The feeling is equally mutual because my learning and growth thrives.

So, what's the problem? The crux of my anxiety is not the energy and effort I've given to others. It's the reality of not investing time in helping myself get unstuck.

Introduction

Truth is, the universe has given me everything that I've allowed myself to receive. Key words... "that I've allowed." Even more, I have not chosen the path of least resistance. I've done the exact opposite. Why haven't I coached and advised myself to success the way I've listened, advised and coached others? Because I've subjected my creativity to the logic of my reasoning mind, and it has worked against me. Thus, I've gone about things the wrong way.

In mild paranoia, I began to question my commitment to personal growth and betterment. Why haven't I found my "bright spot" or, focused on finishing something? How did I choose to go about things the wrong way? Trying to figure it out all at once is the wrong approach, however I chose that route and ended up exactly where I began. Imprisoned by thoughts, where the in-fighting surges and intensifies. Stuck I am.

The Backstory.

Sure, my trusted circle was aware of my love for writing and longing to become a published author.

But, what did that have to do with me taking action and completing my creative pursuits?

Gridlocked by shame and blame, I could never clearly explain (other than high-level procrastination) why my efforts had not resulted in completion of a novel, chapbook or, any published work.

There were those I avoided, who, after hearing me recite poetry or, speak would ask, "Are you published? 'Where can I find your work?" Looking foolish, I'd give the same weak implausible response of, "uh, not yet... but, I'm working on it." Then, in an attempt to make up for my poor response, I'd sheepishly offer my business card and invite them to visit my unfinished website. Talk about feeling sick to my stomach. It's really bad when you fail to convince yourself of your own excuse. I was so embarrassed.

Adding to my inertia, my beloved "cloned" son (the male version of me), cheered me on (bugged me) by reminding me of the numerous unfinished projects I needed to work on. After all, he grew up watching me plant my nose in books, sleep with books, post notes on mirrors, plug my ears for complete silence and constantly write and jot notes of inspiration that created my "when I write my books pile." I was a mess—inside and out.

Somehow, I'd ignored how often I'd guided others through their negative self-talk, about their dreams yet, I hadn't conquered my own. Why was I so helpful, encouraging and motivating to others, but not so great at putting my own plan into action and coaching myself to completion about something I loved? This backwards reality bothered me. I needed to understand why my relationship with myself was the way that it was. Why wasn't I taking care of what I valued? For sure, I loved it. Somehow, I had to get turned around because it was clear that I couldn't get there from here.

What was holding me back? What's not so funny, is well over ten years ago, I purchased the book titled, *What's Really Holding You Back*, by Life Coach, Valorie Burton, attended her seminar and received an autographed copy of her book—read, highlighted and took notes. Above her autograph, she inscribed the word "Persevere!" I journaled about how inspired I was and for sure thought I'd entered momentum. Needless to say, within weeks my efforts stalled, signaling another false start.

What was killing my creative flow? Why was my inner-talk negative, palpable and rock solid? Why'd I get up to bat, but never take a swing? I'm not talking about a hit, just a swing!

Even though I was trying to take action towards the thing I wanted, I was flowing energy towards things I did not want. What does that mean? I was out of sync which created more inner conflict, which is not a natural sustainable state— it's a diversion. An exhausting repetitive one, at that. I was waist deep in "I'll get around to it, someday," mode.

The deeper I thought, the more emotional I became. I felt angry and hurt. I'd let myself down. I realized I was the culprit—the actor, producer and manager of "my story; the cause and effect." No one caused me to go against myself. I'd thwarted and impeded my progress. Again, I had not chosen the path of least resistance. I'd done the exact opposite. I was the roadblock on my path, and through self-defeating habits, I'd become accustomed to being a "would-be" creator.

Introduction

My success was caught in a paralysis that was self-made. And, the space between where I was and where I wanted to be was filled with my stuff. This truth made me really sick to my stomach.

The matter of creating wasn't trivial, but somehow through negative mental chatter I made it trivial. It felt like I was seeking permission and validation from "some source," something that said, yes, she's a writer, an author and her work is worth reading. That source was me. Finally, I saw my role in my mess but still, I didn't know how to reach out to "myself."

It took some time (years) to correct my thinking and to stop trying to swim upstream. I had to dig deep but, I finally got a clearer view.

The landscape and resistors of my mind was loaded with untruths I'd practiced for too long. There was a disconnect between my personal power and what I desired to experience. And, the commitment to my vision only existed in the fantasy of my desire because belief in my ability was weak. I was doing the exact things I'd advised others not to do. This was the seat of my inner turmoil.

Admittedly, I needed some re-work. It was time to commit, work through and get rid of the illusions I'd embraced and served. I had to start (but, this wasn't really the beginning) accepting, valuing and, appreciating what I truly desired, regardless of everything else.

Foolishly, I desired and expected buy-in from others because I felt so inspired through reading and writing. I wanted those I loved to experience "my" enthusiasm. Not, because I believed everyone should love writing, but because of the freedom of how good it feels to be tuned into doing something you love; something that is "you." However, that's not how things work. Everyone is unique and has their own "something" to tune into.

This was my fault because I'd placed more value on the opinion of those I cared about, over the opinion I held of myself as a writer. I fought within saying things like, "nobody cares how important writing is to me." When, I should've been asking and answering, how important is writing to you, De'Broada? My thinking was upside-down, misaligned and the rejection I'd experienced in other areas of my life creeped into my creative, which caused me to second guess my work and develop unrealistic expectations. This was the mess I had to straighten out.

The real beginning was accepting that people are going to think what they're going to think, and there's nothing you can do about it; and that's completely okay. Really. Ergo, "What you think of me is none of my business." What's more important is how and what you think about yourself. And that's where my work began. It took some time, but I found my power base.

What's really going on?
Writing is so much bigger than me. Once I decided to cooperate I was able to align and complete this work.

Change is possible. It's also, exhausting, frustrating and basically the worst-best experience you can endure. This is no secret. What's usually lacking is self-motivation and mental toughness to make change happen. We want change for the better, but we want it uncomplicated with minimal pain, loss of time and resources. And, if it doesn't happen quickly, we talk ourselves out of it.

That was me. I wanted things to change, but I was a high-level procrastinator. I was afraid, hesitant and unwilling (resistant), to make certain sacrifices to create my dream of writing for a living. That's only part of the story.

My circle of trust possessed a similar mindset. You know the saying, "birds of a feather, flock together." Yes, I had full support but, I was communicating with others who were just as skeptical and reluctant as I, about making changes to experience different levels of success. Sure, we had great ideas and shared similar beliefs about success and risk taking; and we supported each other's triumphs and setbacks. However, we were busy managing over-loaded stress induced lives and expressing or, suppressing our emotions, which were mostly negative. By the time, we gave attention to our dreams we were tired and the desire had somewhat diminished.

Another thing we became really good at was discussing disappointment, failure, defeat and hard times; which did not help. Like others, we'd worked hard at maintaining our comfortable monotonous middle-aged lives, but had little hope in change. A fresh start sounded good, but, lacked appeal. There just seemed to be, too much in the way—too many steps, risks etc. However, we remained cautiously optimistic with little fulfillment and lived in "someday" mode. Although we did more talking than taking action we still hoped things would change. After all, we were pessimistically revved up. Poof! Fizzle. In the meantime, we skimped on the planning and took very little action to create our dreams.

These explanations are not to defend or, place blame. They reveal the mindset during that time, which kept me from maintaining the standard I'd held others too. It's no secret, you must act on your dream if you want to experience it.

Obviously, we had control, options and opportunity to change our life. What I didn't notice or, pay attention to was how my pessimistic attitude was actively sabotaging my efforts—every day. I was totally off the mark.

Yes, my faith and belief was strong, but stronger than either of those was fear. Fear of the unknown—real or unreal. I had, what I call mistaken certainty. I was certain of my actions yet, doubtful and I sincerely wanted more. Does this ring true for you?

Moving things around.

Change is hard and facilitating change within is even harder. To be honest, for a long time I sucked at it. Big time.

Life was very challenging until I learned new information, changed my perception and began to manage my emotions in healthier ways. I had to learn not to focus on past problems and situations, to trust myself, and take full responsibility for my happiness. Adding more, the devil was always in the details. When I decided to become more accountable instead of playing victim and justifying my anger, things began to change.

It took a while but, I learned how to truly be myself. The more I became willing to let go of the past and self-created limits, (resistance) my awareness expanded. I achieved a more balanced state of mind and I didn't feel controlled by the highs and lows of emotions, due to life events. And, I learned as we grow spiritually, we become more grounded and are less likely to act out of emotions.

Introduction

I wrote most of this book long ago, but I was so stuck in self-pity, blame and inertia it was difficult for me to finish creating what you are now reading. What I know now and understand is, although the time was difficult, the growth I experienced, shaped and corrected the error in me. Yes, I'd written most of the material but, I was not united with the vision nor, ready for the purpose or, opportunity that was waiting for me.

Ok, so maybe esteem and negative self- talk isn't why you haven't followed through on your dream. Maybe you're running excuse is "I don't have time or, 'Someday I'll get around to it." However, you never have. But, you think about it all the time. How long are you going to keep doing this to yourself? A wise person once said, "Your thoughts will either imprison or liberate you." I agree.

What I want you to know is what you want is still possible. No matter how things seem you can have the life you want. But you must shift your mindset and make room for your desires which requires trust, surrender and letting go. Your dream is possible because you want it.

The wisdom within are conversations or, "home truths" that helped me get a handle on myself and improve my life. And, I am confident they can have the same effect on you. My internal dialogue revealed that I was the limiting factor—the obstacle—the thing in my way. Until, I became aware and realized my writing was dead due to my thinking, I wasn't able to completely produce the work God had given me. Thus, I decided to cooperate and no longer resist this truth. This was easier said than done.

I changed course when I applied the practical advice I received. Honestly, I expected to struggle, but I had to try it out. It actually wasn't as gut wrenching as I'd imagined. It was positive and renewing because I was finally taking steps in the direction of my desire. Inspiration created the momentum and I followed the guidance. This was the first time I aligned my thoughts and actions to create a more enjoyable life experience. Everything we think, affects everything we do. When I decided to do the most important things first, I grew emotionally, spiritually, physically and mentally. Spirit always communicates and give us what we desire. However, we must remain open to see and make use of what we receive.

About this book.

My Way, is my first published work and, of course, I'm proud that I finally put pen to paper for the purpose of creation. This writing touches on things that I had to gain a better understanding of in order to change my mindset. Everybody wants to get from over there to over here. This book will help you do that. It's a simple, easy read and applicable to every day life.

I wrote this book with you in mind because I believe in inspiration and I desire to connect on a spiritual, emotional and intellectual level (whatever that level is for you). And, I want you (reader) to know I understand the experience of being too loyal, too long to the wrong, so let's move on.

Everything within is about communicating and alignment with yourself. It's about getting out of your way. This is *My Way* of saying something about who I am and what I believe. We are from one source and the whole of our intelligence is an interconnected network of things known or, expressed. Each of us, bring energy to the whole. But, most often we don't know or, understand the value of what we bring. Also, most of us live trying to escape mental disharmony and conflict (inner and outer) and experience what we collectively coin as luck—good and bad. Thus, ignoring the fact that we create and choose what we experience every day.

So, to help you, which helps me (through thought, conversation, meditation and inspiration), I encountered the mental obstacles I'd placed in my own way (unknowingly). Overtime, my defeatist mindset and actions created a continuous feeling of being "out of sync and untrue" to myself. My misery was a result of me looking for a happy ending. There is no such thing. If you want to know the ending, check the beginning. I was resisting what I needed to do, which was to take full responsibility for my happiness if I wanted to experience peace and joy.

How to use this book.

The goal is to use this book as a tool or, guide. It will encourage your personal growth, development and help you become your best self.

16

As you read, spend a few minutes and focus on your thoughts. Pay attention to how you relate and respond to the material. Hold the discussions in mind to hear and understand your truths, thoughts and reactions. You must know your patterns and habits before you can change your thinking. My friend, even if you think you're smart or, solid on a topic or, know all there is to know...you're incorrect.

My Way, is broken down into three sections and is most useful in 1) helping you figure out what you want, 2) how to work through your stuff, and 3) how to get out of your way.

The personal discussions are inspiration and wisdom, which provoked my thinking and propelled me forward. Although simplistic and repetitious these "home truths" helped me get out of my way and aligned me with my desire to experience peace, abundance and enjoy life.

The words are unstructured yet, effective. They're not in any pre-defined manner or, model but, they provided the moral guidance needed during my times of frustration and struggle. Study, application and repetition of these "home truths", will create the momentum needed to clean up your mental act and help you get focused.

After each lesson, take time to journal or, write out your thoughts. Discuss or, share with a trusted friend. If you don't have any thoughts, please continue reading. They may come to you later.

The best way to learn, as you move through the discussions is to keep a journal or, notebook. There is a relationship between what you want and what you don't want. And, within that relationship is where we struggle (contrast) and hold ourselves back. You must know how you feel, what you feel, and how you want to feel, before positive change can occur.

Answer any questions contained in the lesson or, that arise thereafter. This will help you recognize your patterns of behavior and thinking and distinguish between your perception and the writer's thought. Before you can change your "stuff" and make better decisions, you must know what habits are creating your "stuff".

Own your behavior. This is about you dealing with "you." Be accountable and responsible, not shameful, guilty or, self-critical. You will not be able to move on until you accept and allow change to happen. This means you will have to release your resistance to change (whatever that change is). Since change is a process, you will repeat this action over and over, and that's okay. This is why I've asked that you read the material over and over.

Change is not instantaneous nor, is transformation. Aligning your behavior and actions with your desires is a process that takes effort, time and patience. I'm sure you agree the process of creating a "new you" carries its own weight and pressure, if you are truly seeking to change.

We all have a fair share of mental cobwebs to clear, so there's no set path. I ask that you think openly, be honest and patient with yourself and receive and apply what you may need. Why? Because you must get to a place where you understand the content (what's behind the feeling) of your emotions because they lead to the choices and decisions you make about your life. Often times, these choices are self-defeating and on auto-pilot.

Introduction

Being so, take time and monitor your thoughts to change behavior and make better decisions. This will align you with what you want and believe. Thus, creating a better life experience. The process is challenging and intensifies as you discover, change and master your thinking. But, this will be some of the most important work you've done for yourself. I trained and coached myself to think differently and made changes to create better outcomes in my life—so can you.

This book is not a substitute for professional help or therapy. If you desire counseling, or help as you grow, take the steps in that direction. It contains the wisdom which helped me move from where I was in my life to where I wanted to be. The one thing I confess, is as I began to study and meditate to further understand my viewpoint, I discovered not only did I have problem "A," but a host of others that were attached to my delusional pattern of thinking. It took work, effort and patience clearing out the weeds but, it was worth it.

I share these notations deliberately, because this is what worked for me. I believe in them and I'm offering it to you. Reading this book will help you. How do I know? Because my desire is to inspire you to action, if you're open to receive. And it's bigger than me.

My hope is to connect with you on the emotional (personal) level because this is the level where things get sorted out. Being in a space of transparency, vulnerability, trust and intimacy with myself helped me achieve clarity and get out of my own way. What you decide to do is your choice. However, you can do and become what you want and live to your full capacity.

May these words arouse, heal, inspire, teach and show you whatever you're in need of. There's no straight path to success, but we can leave the chaos behind and choose not to block the flow. I've left the chaos behind... join me.

Thank you for reading my book.

"Each heart knows its own bitterness, and no one else can fully share its joy." Proverbs 14:10

MY WAY

Finding My Way Back to Me!

"The space between where you are,
where you want to be
And... who you are
and who you want to become
is filled with your stuff."

de 'Broada

ONE

I'm Writing for My Freedom

"Seek first the kingdom of God, above all else, and more will be added to you."

Matt 6:23

One: What Do You Want? (Getting Clear)

I
am the energy of God
I am whole, I am love
I am complete
I am the energy of God
In me there is no defeat

I
am the energy of God
I am whole, I am love
I am complete
I am the energy of God
In me there is no defeat

I
am he, she, me, we, One
I can do, see, believe, become
I don't long to be free
because I am of thee
the whole of his essence
resides in me

Because...
I
am the energy of God
I am whole, I am love
I am complete
I am the energy of God
In me there is no defeat

Rise and Shine!

Oh, my God... where did my life go?

You know you're not satisfied. Your inner voice tells you over and over, something's wrong or missing and you need to change, stop or, start something. Basically, you've got work to do.

If this wasn't so, you wouldn't have received this book. It wouldn't be in your possession nor, would you have been exposed to it. Trust, this is not a coincidence.

You can pretend not to hear the voice speaking to you, but there are reasons these words are coming your way. Just as there are reasons you are in charge of your life. Your brain will always tell you what's wrong because it's designed to survive and thrive.

Let's face it, living life is serious business. Getting better and changing your life does not happen by accident. It's an on purpose intentional action. An action taken by the owner of the life being lived, which is YOU. It's time to roll up your sleeves and get to work creating the life you want. What you want is still possible.

Welcome to the grind.

Attitude

What you learn you also teach.

All thought begins in the mind, so let's start here. I can't begin discussing success, personal development and change without acknowledging that success or, failure depends on your attitude. The attitude you choose will make or, break you. It will add to or, take away from your success because success is a result of how you think. And thoughts reflect attitude, which create our experiences.

Attitude is the storehouse of thoughts and excuses. These thoughts are positive and encouraging or, negative and irrational. Wrong thinking produces discord. This is why you must guard your mind. Allowing unchecked, incorrect information into your mind affect desire, decision and effort. And, often causes undesired long lasting emotional relationships with loneliness, heartache and anger; ending in a rut, or feeling lost. This doesn't have to be your outcome.

There are no walls preventing you from getting what you want. Unless, you're living in confinement and have to wait until time has been served. Life doesn't have to be perfect to get, do and become what you want. There's no such perfect thing. However, you have to get started. Use what you have. Do what you can from where you are. Begin by affecting the things within your control which are your actions, thoughts and behavior.

Changing your life starts with having the right attitude about what you aspire to do, be and become. You know, if you're giving it your all and what attitude you've chosen. Or, if you're going about it the hard way. Is your attitude working for or, against you? Do words like: selfish, stubborn, resistant, mean, immature, lazy, desperate or, failure describe your behavior? If you've chosen the wrong approach, listen to hear the error in your thinking and correct it. What excuses do you tell yourself about why you can't change your life? Do you let yourself off the hook for not taking responsibility for the experiences you create?

A negative attitude will define your behavior and actions and consistently divert you from the path of success. The conflicting beliefs are the cause of distress, contradiction and frustration within.

Thoughts, beliefs, desires and vision need to align. Your energy (thoughts and effort) must align with your goal or, you will struggle over and over. How do you correct this? You must learn to go with the flow. Sounds, cheesy huh? What I mean is, if you are flowing your energy toward things you don't want and trying to take action towards the things you do want...you are not in sync, not aligned and conflict will be the outcome.

So how do you go with the flow? Change your perception, which, is not so easy. Okay, it's not easy. Look at the other side. The good news is, perception belongs to the perceiver which is you. And, you can change it any time because every day is a new moment to perceive differently.

I'd decided and perceived incorrectly and was not at peace. So, I had to decide again. Like me, many of you have disrupted your success by thinking incorrectly. Check your mood and adjust your attitude.

Choose success.

Self-Awareness

Choose You

When you're not comfortable putting your needs first, it is difficult to know what you want. Over time, you can grow away from thinking about your desires and believe doing so, is selfish. When you stop listening to your desires, they seem to fade. This causes inner conflict and uncertainty. And the struggle with guilt and self-pity begin to peak. The result, living a passionless life.

In order to create the life you want, you must become self-aware. What is self-awareness? Knowing who you are, what you want and don't want, believing you deserve it and, that it's possible.

Knowing who you are doesn't mean describing what you do—occupation. More so, who are you behind what you do? How do you see and feel about yourself? How do you treat yourself—mind, body and spirit? What are your values? What do you want? Do you believe in yourself?

Self-awareness is the working foundation of dreams and relies on confidence. And, confidence grows as you get out of your comfort zone and act on your beliefs.

There are a lot of things we do but, can't explain why we do them, which doesn't make sense. Stop functioning out of conformity of doing things you were taught without question. Especially, when it doesn't add value to your experience. Think and ask yourself why to better understand and become aware of your behavior. What do you need to let go of, stop doing or change? What road are you traveling on? Peace, joy, anger, frustration. Examine your life. You own it and owe it to yourself.

Become aware.

Life

The predictable outcome.

The sun rises and sets, the moon glows. Seasons follow a pattern... winter comes after fall, day turns into night... tides roll in and back out. Life remains. Life is here to serve you. It will give you what you ask of it.

If you want to change, you can. You are in charge of your life. Life allows you to call the shots. Therefore, if you want your life to change, it will change when "you" decide to change. If not, it will continue pretty much the same as it has been. Complaining, wishing, hoping and waiting only result in the passing of time—not the changes you seek.

Don't waste your opportunity by not deciding to act. Don't become good at doing nothing. **Create the life you want.** What do you want from it?

Don't be passive. Live with intention.

Time

I am the boss of me.

You are the boss of you. You are the owner and manager of your time, energy, effort and motivation. Each day the

Creator grants 86,400 seconds without any request from you. It is given to all—young, old, rich, poor, beggar, thief, white, black, brown etc.

We're granted time for a purpose; not every second holds the same worth. Don't compromise your value by taking time for granted. Learn and practice using time productively. Choose to act everyday towards your desires.

Time is a brief opportunity to take action. Pay attention and take advantage of the opportune times and seasons. One of the worst things you can do is waste it. The uncompromised misery is once the day cycles through it's gone. We have a limited amount of time in the physical. Each day we're all walking towards the same end.

Time is a gift that waits for no one. It cooperates with creation and will deliver to you exactly what you ask of it. Don't get in your own way.

The clock runs out.

Personal Development

Who are you becoming?

Personal development is one of the most challenging things you will do over the course of your life. Why? Because you are the only one who can raise or lower your standard and dealing with yourself is work. Becoming who you say you are, not who others say you are is a laborious on-going process—mentally, physically, emotionally and spiritually.

Becoming better requires you to make decisions, put forth effort, be determined, replace excuses, learn something new and deal with adversity and change in positive ways. Changing habits and correcting your judgment to become a better "you" takes a lot of time and actions. The work is constant. You have to become your reason and inspiration; push, pull and encourage yourself. Yes, there are setbacks, bad spots and restarts. But, if you clarify your goal at the beginning, your outcome will be better determined and where you need strength, you can become strong.

Learning and development may compare to others, but you will only see your experience from your world and that's okay because you do not need to have the same experiences to grow. But, to change your condition, you must continue growing. So, decide, commit, act, succeed and repeat. You are worth it!

I am worth the changes I seek.

Fear

Everyday

Everyday there are conflicts and miracles. And doubt is normal. Beware, the voice of self-doubt and uncertainty will always be waiting to greet you because it is your voice. It's internal. It's your fear. You have to overcome this enemy if you plan on living a successful life.

Fear is an opponent you can't see but for sure you can hear. To keep fear under your feet, do not preoccupy your mind with past thoughts. You have to choose to listen to your other voice and keep this enemy off of your heels. Remember, the mental battlefield is where you grind it out. No matter your perception, every day you are in a battle for your mind and the gift of time. Fear has to be cultivated to become strong. Its strategy is to create stagnation, inertia—waste your life. Don't give fear power in your life. God is with you wherever you go.

How do you know when you're operating in fear? When you become, afraid and believe there is another will at work (an attack or, threat) real or, imagined and take things personal. You function in fear when you're in anxiety-provoking situations; around offending events or personalities or, just have negative, unloving thoughts about life, people or situations.

You must practice finding your peace because unloving thoughts about anything will keep you in the hell your fear has created. And, this hell will follow you wherever you go. This is because you are the "carrier" of your disharmony. Do not create an allegiance to fear; keep it at bay. Don't allow it to trick you into believing your peace is destroyed.

It is okay to have fear. It is not okay for fear
to have me.

Pessimism

Cynic.

Are you difficult, unhappy, untrusting and disagreeable most of the time? Are you mean or, passive, aggressive? If so, why? Where's the hurt? What has you so upset and irritable? You must uncover this before you can pursue anything.

If your overall perception or, outlook on life is pessimistic you can forget about being successful. The purpose of pessimism is to keep you living in fear. It is a belief in darkness over light—refusing to let light enter.

This is completely opposite of the purpose of life, which is joy.

When your normal experience is defeat and defense, dissatisfaction is the outcome. A defeatist attitude does not lead to a fabulous life experience. Just like an unhappy life will never lead to a happy ending. If this is your struggle, correct the error in your mind. Otherwise, you're on the road leading "nowhere."

Negative experiences require energy and must be pursued. Are you drawn to the negative? Do you trust anyone? Are you addicted to negative persuasion or, influences? Have you chosen an attitude of indifference?

Indifference is choosing to stay in perpetual pessimism, see opportunities as problems and thrive off of the negative. Basically, the absence of appreciation for life; thus, ensuring you stay in the same dead space. Know that, whatever you choose will serve its full purpose. However, you can correct this thinking and rescue yourself from your own grip.

Yes, we're designed to live fruitful lives. But, success is not a happenstance. God will put it within your reach, but you must want and work for it. Overcoming pessimism is hard and it requires a deep desire—hunger—for a better life experience. Without a hunger for something more—

spiritual, physical, emotional or, mentally—the life experience becomes inactive and unfeeling.

You have the willpower to change your life. All choices lead somewhere—peace, joy, chaos or, disaster. Select a road that lead to "somewhere." It is your responsibility to make the invisible visible in your life. Don't be the journey that never got started.

Why have faith in the negative?

Responsibility

You are the star.

Responsibility is tough stuff. No matter the circumstance, you have a role in the life you are living. Matter of fact, it's your life movie and you are the star. If you don't like it, you can revise the script at any time. First, you must take full responsibility for it. Again, blaming and complaining will not change anything. Blame only ensures the elapse of time.

Why isn't the quality of your life the way you want? More than likely, it's because you're consistently doing or, not doing things that lead to where you don't want to be. What have you done to create the life you say you want?

Before you can experience it, you must know what you really want. Is it better health, relationship, job, finances?

There's no particular starting point. Start from where you are. Begin with your attitude about responsibility. Many of us believe we're entitled to a good life and we are. What we choose to ignore is the responsibility for creating a good life belongs to each person. I would like_____, to happen in my life.

You are responsible for your happiness.

Accountability

You have to fix your own life.

Accountability is answerability. You must answer, acknowledge and assume responsibility for your actions or, lack of action. There's no way around it. Like it or not.

Types of accountability. Positive accountability lead to POWERFUL changes in your life. Positive accountability is demonstrated by acknowledging reality, owning and accepting responsibility, seeking and finding solutions and taking action to make things happen in your life.

Negative accountability lead to victim behavior and thinking, POWERLESSNESS. Negative accountability is demonstrated by behaving unaware, example, "I don't know," blaming others for your outcomes, having an "I can't" mindset, not taking action and waiting for someone or, something to change your life. As a victim, you allow and practice wrong things. You function in a state of denial—knowing, ignoring and pretending things are not as bad as they really are. You know when you're out of control. Seek help if you need it. When you run away from your problems they simply run after you. It is never too late because you are worth it.

Answer your why's and destroy your lies.

Truth

Truth is contrary to reality

What you choose to believe is decided by you. Know that a steady flow of misinformation and misdirection can overwhelm the truth, making it seem as though what is true, is not. Perception changes, truth doesn't.

Always seek the truth. You've heard, seek the truth because the truth will set you free. Just know when doing so, you will have to deal with your past which can be emotionally painful. However, healing and transformation is within.

If you have a problem with being honest, you will not be comfortable or, able to communicate truthfully. You must be able to be honest with yourself first, to practice integrity. Something as simple as, saying, "yes or no", when that is your truth must be a comfortable space for you.

We create so many problems when we avoid being honest about how we feel or, how something affects us. Often, we give the "safe" response instead of being clear and concise. This is a waste of time because you cannot eliminate distress of the unknown by responding with uncertainty; especially when dealing with yourself. If this is your stance, you might as well stick your head back inside your turtle shell. Stop looking for the easy way out. Learn to speak your truth. It will increase your self-respect from within.

What you accept to believe as true, becomes true. And, your behaviors reveal your understanding of that truth. Many lies and old beliefs are passed from one generation to the next and accepted as truth. This is very dangerous. Guard your mind.

Omission is a lie because it's selective deception. Being taught or, told something over and over can cause you to think it is true. And once you believe a lie it is difficult to discard or, unlearn. Investigate the illusions before they

41

become inescapable. Sometimes this may require a deeper understanding of truth than you're accustomed to.

Everyone has a heartbreaking story to tell. When you experience truth, you can hear lies clearly. Your intuition will guide you. Truth, being what it is, will free you from everything it is not. Tell yourself the truth so you can accept and release what is of no benefit to you. When you practice integrity, you will not be offended when you hear others speak truthfully. Truth teaches us how to serve our own best interest.

I am not what happened to me.

Past

Make peace with your past.

No one likes being reminded of a negative past. Guilt and shame are hell and offer no consolation or, escape. Even so, there will always be those who will define you by past mistakes. This energy is toxic to emotional and spiritual health.

Some may focus on your past more than present without acknowledging they've traveled on the same self-road. And, downplay the positive changes you've made. Perhaps, they didn't agree with your choices. Or, they didn't think you'd be able to overcome and rise above obstacles and escape disaster. Does this mean they're judgmental? Yes, we all are. You will always experience being judged by others. This isn't a crime it's part of the human condition. We all judge. You're doing it right now. When we judge, we're speaking from our place of awareness and experience, not others. None of us see the world the same. We're equal in God's love but, our perspectives differ.

Real-talk, no one has the exact same perspectives, values nor, enthusiasm as you. Just as no one has the same fingerprint. Learn to see it for what it is—difference. Disagreement or, conflict isn't always about someone trying to break you down or, jack up your life. Stop personalizing others motivations. If someone is seeking to hurt you intentionally, end the toxic relationship.

Remember, we all have equal amounts of constant crap going on in our lives. Just like you're working out your stuff, so are they. Is what the person think of you more important than what you think of yourself? If not, why do you have inner-discontent? Why is your peace disturbed? Check yourself. Just because we're not walking around in each other's shoes, doesn't mean our destination isn't the same. This is correct but still, no matter how tough-skinned you are, no one appreciates being spoken of in a negative manner.   Just as no one likes being slapped in the face. Agree?

Judgment is painful because it lacks compassion, understanding and forgiveness. It hurts and feels like attack and punishment from someone you love. The silly part is, even if they played a role and manipulated your vulnerability they may still find you at fault. This is toxic. The belief behind the madness is possibly a thought or, feeling of them being mistreated during your struggle, which led to unchecked anger. They may even credit themselves with your success, even though you may've felt unsupported during your time of need. Maybe they think you owe them. For what? Time spent. There is no compensation. Careful, this trap will create feelings of indebtedness, activate and fuel anger. What's done is done.

This is hard. So, what's really going on here? The work you're doing should be on you, not on trying to change the behaviors of others.   That's an immediate lost cause, and why you keep "running off the road." Remember, you're on the path of changing you, not others.

So, how do you keep from planting seeds of disharmony, in your life, and free yourself from being preoccupied with this drama? Confront and cuss people out. Wrong answer. However, that may be your burning desire. What must happen is, you have to learn to handle problems from a different perspective. It sounds simple, but we fail so often at it. What you must learn to do is, let people be people. Allow them to be as perfectly flawed as you are and move on with life. Why waste time and energy being mad or, hurt about what you cannot control? That's not what you want to hear, right?

Focus on yourself. Start here. What is your connection with your past? Do you still have shame about it? Are there secrets? Your past can only have power over you if you have an allegiance to it. If you know you're better than your mess, then give it less attention. Do you define yourself by what others think of you? How do you see yourself? Are you seeking the approval of others? Do you still tell the story of what happened to you? Have you forgiven yourself? If not, you're not alone.

Most times we're not hurt or, angry for the reasons we think. Forgive yourself, let go (release, not resign), and move forward. Once you do, you will be able to move freely and not be affected by what someone else may think of you. Stick to your standard. Elevate your thinking. Move on and stop looking back. Everyone has messed up, needed and received help.

Move beyond negative energy peacefully. In you have a debt, settle it. Apologize sincerely, show gratitude for the support received and move on. Do not invest energy or, you will end up depleted, exasperated and frustrated. Control what you can.

You can't control what others think.

Pardon me please?

We're all fragile beings.

There's no denying, we paint the picture others see. So, before finding fault, own the image you project. This does not mean to live in your past. It means, be honest about what or, how you've taught others to think of and treat you. If you're doing all of the work, being disrespected or, mistreated by someone, take a step back and see your role in "allowing" the disrespectful behavior to occur. Yes, you are a participator.

Own your stuff. When you do, don't downplay or be dismissive about the affect your past actions had on love ones. This too, is offensive. Particularly, the impact on those who supported or, depended on you during your struggle. Being offended is a shared response because the pain of an experience is never only on one side. Acknowledge the reason for their frustration, but don't create a sanctuary for guilt. Move on.

We all belong to the Creator. Being so, accept that those you've hurt may have anger, resentment or, feel mistreated and disrespected. Whether real or imagined this must be dealt with. Take a closer look at yourself not the problem.

Reality is, if someone experienced hell through your actions and behavior they're not sitting around saying, "that wasn't so bad, can we continue?" Sure, they may have forgiven you, however forgetting the pain is not an easy feat. Everyone looks out for the most precious commodity (self), and try to avoid pain. Contemplate what you are accusing others of and ask yourself, "What did I bring to the situation that hurt or, disappointed my love ones?" You must see sameness (in others) to correct perception and offer forgiveness. Again, we're not walking around in each other's shoes.

The point is to offer an apology just as you'd like to receive one. It's not easy, right? We've all experienced failure and success and been judged for it. Practice putting down the sword and work on your faultfinding. Treat others in the manner you want to be treated. "Judge not, and you will not be judged; condemn not, and you will not be condemned; forgive, and you will be forgiven...for with the measure you use it will be measured back to you." (Luke 6: 37-38). If you have resentment towards a person you want to be free of, release yourself from being angry with them.

Forgiveness changes your heart.

What do you want?

I don't know.

It's your job to know what you want and figure out how to achieve it. Where do you stand in relationship to what you say you want? Are you shrugging your shoulders as saying, "I don't know?" If you don't know, who does? What's in the way of you knowing? Do you function in negative expectation? Meaning, you don't know what you want because you don't believe what you want is possible. No matter how comfortable, that's not a place to camp out. You need to decide and move towards it.

How can you decide what you want when life is full of stress and responsibilities? Life is life. Such a response is a deflection from dealing with the truth of the matter. All life has purpose, but you must see the purpose for your life over the purpose you have given it in your mind. That purpose is to achieve joy. Sounds like a load of crap, huh?

Don't allow the thing you serve bind you. Listen from within and pay attention to the signals. You have a guide. The constant, uncomfortable low vibration of dissatisfaction with your life quality, is the indicator and precursor to change. The creator always tells you when you're out of balance, stressed, and unhappy. This is when you need to figure things out; to get things done. It's choice time.

Knowing what you don't want to experience, tells you what you do want to experience. What do you want to experience? How do you want to live? Remember, time in the physical does run out.

The Creator's energy is in all creations. Problems and answers are together, but you must recognize the problem to solve it. Start by changing your mind and attitude and thousands of steps will follow. Identify what you want to experience, believe it's possible and take action towards it. You must get outside of your comfort zone to create it. Until you do, you will stay stuck in your chosen dilemma.

Here's an assist.

Do you prefer feeling good over not feeling good? What does that look like? What does your world look like when you're feeling good? What are you doing? Who's involved? Where are you (place, time, location)? When you can describe clearly what feeling good looks like, you will be able to see what you love.

I used to make it so hard because I was looking for a specific thing but, I really wanted to experience feeling good about whatever I was doing because there are so many things that I enjoy doing. What I'm saying is, there isn't one specific thing. For example, I feel good when I exercise, read, write, spend time with family and good friends, laugh, relax, learn, talk to young people, listen to music, travel, go out to dinner etc. When you figure out what gives you, your good "vibrations" and do more of that, you will begin tuning in to what you want and like to do.

Do you want to sing, dance, serve others, cook, study, teach, mentor, play sports, draw, make people laugh? Are you drawn to animals, ministry, nature, places, things, science, technology, medicine, government the elderly? What do you feel good doing? How can you get more of that in your life? That is the feeling you want to align yourself to. Your good feeling will create a good attitude and more good vibrations which lead to a good day, and good days create a good life experience. Don't try hard at becoming something, just be you.

You are the answer to your problem.

I Don't Know

You do...listen within.

I get it. Perhaps, you don't want to know. Or, it feels overwhelming or, too complicated when you think about your life situation and you end up feeling frustrated. Maybe, you don't want to think because change is hard and you expect to struggle. Do you feel stuck in your chosen hell—sadness, anger, apathy?

Listen, everyone is working through some type of pain. Be reminded, feelings and emotions are signals but, they are perception based. Often, when you stay in a negative space (mentally), you grow and become uninspired and out of touch with your authentic self. Then you turn on yourself like you've forgotten what makes you smile. You say things like I don't know what I like; I don't know what I want; I don't know what to do. You're dissatisfied and you certainly know why. You may not admit it, but you know why.

Often, "I don't know" is a response given out of fear. Work on stopping yourself from saying, "I don't know." When you say, "I don't know what to do," the answer is...do that which you do not want to do. You're the thinker of the thoughts. And it's your life. Who should know, if not you?

To get out of this place of unsureness make two lists. On one list, write everything you don't want and on the other list write everything you do want, and compare.

My point is, you are aware of what you want but you've created such static and allowed what you've experienced thus far to change it and get you off course. So, now you don't believe or, feel like you don't know anything anymore. You cannot "not" know. You can be bored, resist or, deny what you know, but you do know.

You ask, why would I resist or, deny knowing? Because when you admit that you know what's wrong, missing, or, desired it creates a feeling of responsibility and you don't want to feel responsible especially, when you've messed up our life. We prefer, "Blame Street, or Not my Fault Avenue," and pretend or, wish things would change. We run from our problems and get angry when they're not solved. Silliness.

Once you tell yourself the truth about what you want and allow yourself to experience the desire (mentally) of it, you "cannot" not want what you want. Read that again. Why? Because who you are inside knows exactly what you want. So, listen within, become transparent and truthful with yourself. You have a guide.

Do you want to go to college, quit smoking, start a business, get married, divorced, lose weight, change jobs, join the military, relocate, save money, have a family, etc.? Decide so you can act. The choice is clear, change your negative mind-script or, stay in a fixed state of disharmony.

You must solve your problem.

Change

You know you need to.

You know you need to change. We all do in some area of our life. The problem is we don't want to because we hate the experience of it. Let me say it in a softer manner. What we lack is the desire and action required to make change happen. We want change to happen but don't want the full responsibility of making change occur. Does that sound better?

Listen, there's no way to ride a horse without getting on it. Change means exactly what it implies. You have to modify, correct or improve what you are doing to raise your current standard. Do things differently. We all know winners win, and losers lose. Where are you in relation to that statement. There's no gray area. Your everyday actions are contributing to the wins or losses in your life. Take a minute and think it over. Are you sick of your current situation or, ignoring it?

Being honest, becoming frustrated (sick and tired) with your current situation can propel you to take action. Also, being backed in a corner has the same effect. I was sick of the situation I'd created in my work life. Yes, I was successful but un-fulfilled. My life was good. I wanted great. So, I decided to do something about it besides roll my eyes and complain. I chose to change.

No matter your circumstance you can always raise the bar, but you must get your mind right. Change begins in the mind. The mental action must be present before the physical can be executed or, prepare to fail. And no, it's not easy. Not ever. Don't believe the lies or, infomercials or, the know-it-all at the job that thinks he knows everything. You will have to be disciplined, committed, put in work (effort), give up time and sacrifice some of your current wants. Honestly, you're going to hate it. But, once you take your thumb out of your mouth and stand on your own two feet, you will be fine. How can I say that better? Once you commit, you will reap the rewards of your efforts. If not, you'll repeat your story. Also, expect the unexpected. This means expect to be challenged. Life will pull the rug from underneath you when you least expect it. Overcoming challenges definitely lead to change.

Where are you on the resistance scale? Is your level of resistance pretty solid? Or, do you maintain a "I know I need to, but eh...I just don't feel like it" attitude? Be careful getting on the road to failure. Being forced to change is a much more unpleasant experience than choosing to change. The "old you" will do everything in its power to prevent any new habits from forming. Especially when the change is something good for you. Why? Because habits are well established and anchored in your comfort zone. Habit is very comfortable and the change you seek is not just going to happen. You've got to find a way to deal with your life circumstance, especially if it causes you pain.

Change is difficult often because you don't know where to begin. Changing your mindset is hard work. It can be like cleaning a dirty house, there's crap everywhere, and you don't know where to start. As anxiety kicks you feel overwhelmed and throttle back; thus, throwing in the towel before you ever get started. Yes, it's a mess. So, what do you do?

First, don't expect easy or, be in a race for the bottom.   Then, begin with what's causing you the most stress. Break the problem down. What are you seeking to change? Is it your finances, health, house, job, relationship or children? One step at a time. There is an end in sight.

I will get better, stronger and smarter than I am right now.

How Do I Change?

Read, Learn, Listen, Do.

Start from where you are. Acknowledge God, his greatness and abundance then you can begin the work of embracing who you are and the plan for your life.

Before you can change your life, you must believe in your potential and expect what you want to come true. And, you must help yourself get better, stronger, smarter than you are now. Become who you desire to be because there is no escaping it. Read, learn, listen and do what you "do not" want to do, but know you should do.   Don't cry and beg for things to change. Or, blame your lack of action on waiting for a sign from heaven. Commit to changing. There's no way around it.

Drama is exhausting and counterproductive. Choose not to get caught up in it or, be the source of creating it. When you resist change, no matter large or small, you become the obstacle in the way of progress.

Complaining, resisting, excuses and laziness are sure ways to waste time and opportunity. These are rooted in fear. No one starts or, stops you but "you."

We can all get our crap under control. Start by accepting that fact. Do not compromise with the adversary, you will lose every time. If you're living in a stressful situation, change will not appeal to you until you become absolutely sick of the pain from choosing to live in it. Once that occurs, you will be open to the idea to change. However, you may respond drastically. Get your behavior under control. If not, anxiety will be your friend and you'll remain in your chosen circumstance. It's really that simple. Regardless, of what you decide the opportunity for peace awaits your choosing of it. God always waits for us to get our crap together.

Don't try to change everything all at once. When you raise, your standard, focus on how you feel and what you see. But, be mindful that there will be moments where change may not feel good and that's okay because it's part of getting to where you're going. You've got to get rid of what you don't need and sometimes the work of loading and unloading is painful. Be of good courage. You're on your way.

Measure your progress by looking at the results the small changes are making in your life. If it's the right behavior do it. You control how high or, low you go. Don't practice the habit of failure by choosing to cut corners, cheat, or set unrealistic expectations (losing 60 pounds in 60 days). Change requires new habits and new habits take time to build.

How do I get out of my way? Do that which you do not want to do. Truth is, change is a frustrating repeated process that seems un-ending. Motivation helps, it's like a treat but it wanes. And repetition is definitely a pain especially when your "I don't want to" mindset is in full effect.

When you feel frustrated, unclear and uncertain about which path or action to take, quiet yourself. Move away from thinking about what to do (in your mind) for a short period of time. When you no longer feel the anxiety, reengage. Listen to your thoughts without all of the extra emotion (drama), and look at both paths to see which line up with how you say want to feel and what you would like to experience. This may take a few attempts but it should be the good stuff. Both paths are not going to be in alignment with what you say you truly desire. This is hard work. Undoing and relearning takes time because you are breaking cycles and changing patterns. You have to think differently to respond differently. Be patient. Remember, growth follows knowledge, action follows inspiration and opportunity follows perception.

Get out of your way.

Comfort Zone

The cost of staying stuck.

Comfort zone is your boring safe zone. Get outside of it so you can grow! You're in your comfort zone when you make excuses instead of doing what you truly want. You tell yourself you are content and satisfied with your quality of life but, feel trapped. Or, you run from the misery you've created and pretend all is well, as you slip further into your circumstance mainly because you just don't want to deal with it.

Fear creates conflicted feelings between who you are and who you want to become. Not to mention, we're also busy trying to be who others want us to be. Instead of figuring things out, you settle. We all experience this.

Comfort and familiarity is tough to overcome because you've probably been operating in it from a very early age. Fear and excuses are passed on from generation to generation through roles, responsibilities and tradition. Even knowing this does not justify making excuses or, belittling yourself to avoid taking action.

Yes, it's a good thing to know where some of your habits and pattern stem from, but it's not a good thing to settle, reinforce and commit yourself to behaviors you've established with people, places or, things that cause you to quit on yourself or, neglect your happiness. Settling causes strife and often feelings of resentment and anger.

Open your eyes (listen within) to see if this is your predicament. Overcoming the stuff in your mind (mind-stuff) and arousing dormant desires will require a lot of effort, but it can be done.

First, decide and commit to change and to stop making excuses. Tell yourself to stop making excuses about how you feel about what you are or, aren't doing. Learn and practice speaking your truth. You will be amazed at the relief you will experience when you respect and speak up for yourself. This is not gender specific. We all have situations we avoid because of our desire to coexist peacefully, thus we settle. Don't confuse settling with compromising, they're not the same.

Don't ignore yourself. Find like-minded people or, a person to share your ideas with that will hold you accountable. We often cry "to have" but never cry "to be." If you have a great idea, go beyond initial enthusiasm and honor your word. Train your brain (willpower) to do what you tell it to do. Become good at taking action and follow-through. Don't create barriers of fear if you make a mistake. Mistakes will happen. Get uncomfortable. When you learn to forget yourself (ego) you can become yourself. If you hold yourself back, you'll never reach your goal.

Do you struggle with the "Big R," Resistance? What's really going on? Are you defending an inferior or, mediocre mindset? Are you concerned about what others will think or say? Are you secretly competing against others? The root of these perceptions is pride. Don't get caught in a misplaced sense of self-worth. Over-inflated, over-valued thoughts and unending self-celebration evolve from pride and unhealthy esteem. Feeling proud and behaving prideful are two different things. Know the difference.

What's your current state of mess? Are you the one doing all of the housework, paying all of the bills, tackling all of the projects? Is there something you want to do but can't find the time or, motivation but deep inside you become depressed or, discouraged when you think of it? Or, does it just feel like something's missing?

You have potential power within.

61

Let Go

Letting go is a choice.

It's really hard to stop clinging to realities that tear your life apart. But you must let go. Avoid comforting or deceiving yourself with excuses and lies or, you'll begin to believe them and create your own misery. Listen within.

You don't need your past anymore so, stop over identifying with it. It's behind you and you can't change it. Stop telling the story of what happened to you if it's not beneficial to someone else. Healing and moving on takes time. But, you must believe you have the power to move on before you can experience it. Let go of the control you think you have over situations. Otherwise, you invite stress into your mess.

Pain is everywhere and will always be an unwanted, faithful friend. Everyone has been hurt. No matter the age, many still suffer from disappointed love from another (parent, child, other) that left them cold, bitter and melancholy. Often, others have moved on from the experience you're still anguished about. Mental replay of hurt leads to depressive thought patterns and the absence of personal power. Don't present yourself as a victim to the world. Decide to release yourself from victim thinking. You are a survivor and need something different now. Seek help if you need it.

Respect your gift of life. Don't allow rejection, anger, guilt, pride or, any other emotion consume your thoughts. Do not choose to sit in rage or, despair. Call who you need to call. Visit who you need to visit. Talk to who you need to talk to. Do not withhold forgiveness. That's self-punishment. Learn the lesson. Forgive yourself and others.

Let go of material things that are no use or, value. Give away or, sell items. Clear your space so, you can clear your mind. When you have too much clutter in your life you can't concentrate or, think clearly. Clutter creates anxiety, which is stress. Get rid of clutter and you will become more relaxed and productive. You must release the old, to receive the new. Choose to become stronger and victorious.

Sometimes letting go means grieving over what isn't and pushing yourself forward to accept what is. Loosen your grip and unclench your fist when it comes to wanting to be right, having the last word, controlling the outcome and only doing things your way. You are not the "guru" of knowing the right way of doing everything. Yes, it may suck but, being energetically married to the outcome of a situation you can't control sucks more. Relax.

There's freedom in release.

Vulnerable

Grow... Become vulnerable.

To grow you must face your fears—be vulnerable. How do you begin to heal and not store the things that have happened to you? How do you shed the skin of your past? Again, the process involves letting go—on a deeper level.

Before you can rule and rise above the error of your ego, you must accept and understand the light, darkness and fear within. You must learn to let go of unloving situations, adverse thoughts and conditions—anger, fear, rejection, worry, envy, sadness, hatred, unrest, etc. We all have fear, but opposite of fear is your desire.

Correct error with truth. Truth will show you where you are in relation to where you want to be. This is the process of alignment. You have to realize you deserve better before you can do better. This is where being vulnerable is helpful. How? By accepting the truth about your life, and making the decision to correct it, you are no longer intimidated by the error in it. Once you accept and forgive yourself for falling short in whatever area, you'll gain clarity and freedom from self-judgment and self-imposed limitations. And you will be able to see where your reality lines up with your aspirations. Vulnerability is all about helping you help yourself.

Do not panic or, be deceived. Risk, reward, rejection and disappointment are all part of being vulnerable. Systems, people and processes will fail you. See mistakes as mistakes and begin again. It's all about you. Learn to adjust and deal with conflict and failure and move on. Get uncomfortable to get your life under control and stop wondering if what you want is possible.

Control, practice and concentrate.

Moving On

The proof of desire is within pursuit.

The process of growth requires you to keep moving and allowing. However, you can only receive as much as you allow within your experience. Remain open to the good.

Living involves risk and pain. Everyone experiences disappointment, rejection, heartache, loss and defeat throughout their journey. Unfortunately, we're limited in our ability to protect ourselves and those we love from the pain associated with taking risk; even when it's an acceptable risk. Thus, you must pursue what you want in spite of being knocked on your behind by life. Why? Because the only way to keep from going backward is to keep moving forward.

I've experienced many setbacks and painfully witnessed the same in the lives of others. Getting knocked down, rolled over, kicked in the shorts emotionally, spiritually, physically and mentally is simply part of the process. The setback and frustration of not being able to create or, become what you want when you want it, is challenging and personal. It's not a welcomed experience. But, you can learn how to respond to it. As my son says, "You must be able to roll with the punches." If not, the built-in antagonist called frustration will convince you to quit on yourself. The quitting I'm referring to is to give up due to frustration, even though you have not achieved your desired goal. Quitting, moving on and choosing something else is your choice. Just be sure it's what you want. Only you know where you stand in relationship to what you say you want.

Maintaining progress requires shifts in attitude, mindset and persistence to pursue what you believe and not give up hope. Relying on inner strength and accepting consequences associated with risk taking is not an easy strength to develop. It takes time and effort. How do you achieve this? You must learn how to take yourself out of the middle to overcome long periods of stress, anxiety and worry.

We all have an attitude of self-righteousness. We want pros and cons and pluses and minuses all spelled out before we stick our toe into the water. We want situations to adjust to our level of comfort. This is the silliness that boxes you in. However, the sooner you free yourself of the "world according to my terms" mentality, the better you'll be able to cope and adjust to what's really going on. Again, get your crap under control, snap out of it and move forward.

Is perfectionism your issue? Perfectionism is fear based thinking because it's driven by the desire to eliminate as many possible negative outcomes regarding a situation before it even happens. The behavior is demonstrated by redoing and rechecking in false hope of reducing or lowering the impact or margin for error. It's a waste of the gift of time.

Truthfully, perfectionism makes things harder than they have to be. It is a pattern of disturbance wherein you create a negative habit of double-triple checking, verifying and preparing to prevent something that you have no control over. How can you control the negative parts of an outcome that you have no control over? Learn to trust, release and allow.

Are you unable to move on because things have not been done your way? Are you shooting for a certain kind of experience? This type of thinking has no end. Are you waiting for someone else's decision to figure out your life? Or, do you struggle with waiting to "feel" like moving on as your life tanks. Frankly, this is the common bs (bull-ritos and shal-sa) that keeps you stuck. When you're living in mess everybody can see it (even when you hide).

No matter what, every day is a gift and an opportunity to move beyond what happened the day before. If you don't take risk, you don't create chance. So, keep moving. Don't get caught up in yesterday. It's over. Raise your thoughts to a higher viewpoint to let go of fear-based thinking. This ensure growth. It took me a while to develop this strength. However, watching my son's courage in taking risk, accepting outcomes and moving on consistently inspired me to continue my pursuit of happiness.

Move through the crap.

Remember These Things

Thoughts and things.

- Think and behave wisely; consequences are always certain.
- Do not create situations in life that aren't good for you.
- Do not create blockages through resistance and self-counsel.
- If you have a solution to a problem, apply it; take the action you can.
- If you do not have a solution do not create chaos by worrying.
- Surround yourself with those who support and allow you to be you.
- How you respond to circumstances is your chosen stress.
- Practice concentration; put your mind on your work daily.
- Have faith, confidence and belief in your potential.
- Expect what you desire to come true.
- Expect the unexpected; there's always more than one possible outcome.

- Guard and train your mind; replace destructive thoughts and thinking.
- Pick yourself up, move through pain and stay true to yourself.

Never give up. Press forward.

TWO

I'm Overcoming My Weaknesses

Wisdom is the principal thing therefore, get wisdom; and with all thy getting get understanding.

Proverbs 4:7

We must feed the mind with a new seed before discontent breeds—De'Broada

The guidance I receive
seems meaningless to me
I say I know God
but doubt his certainty
I really don't want to know
the father's will for me
I like seeing the world
the way I perceive it to be
~~

We're all sick
operating from
encounters and tricks
manipulated version of reality
conformed to logic mentality
low absurd sophisticated
we sound
as we judge creation
when no man was around
~~

through introspection
I realize
I don't know myself
choices made
not in my best interest
centered on me
what to experience
how I want to be
no fraud no fake
just don't know
who I am
I learn from mistake

False Starts and Repeats

Overcoming Weakness

I didn't realize my false starts and repeats occurred because I was overcoming weaknesses. I've have been in a fight with myself. My natural, lazy man has battled my will. All of this time, I've been on the backside of my strength thinking there was an opponent, an opposing obstacle I needed to defeat. But, it's really "me against me." What I know and believe, verses, what I've been taught, conditioned and choose to perceive.

Truthfully, it's harder to work on myself than to work on my problem because I am the cause of the problem. At times, it's been terrible because I'm not good at solving the problem when the problem is me. To conquer, I must understand the truth of my situation not the comfortable version I've told tell myself. This means I have to go back (which is something I really hate) so, I can move forward. Therefore, I must get real personal with myself and not half-ass it. This isn't to find fault, but to understand "why do I keep ending up in the bushes when I drive?"

When you're going through your stuff, trial or test, is this a repeat? Is this the second, third or tenth time?

What lessons are you not getting? Certainly, the message is flashing across the board. What are you trying to control or, force to happen your way? You are the only problem you will ever have. You also are the solution. Lessons are repeated until we get them. Stop shrugging your shoulders and acting like it's someone else's job to fix your life. That's nonsense. Don't wait for things to get worse because they will. Begin again.

Mental Re-work

Perfectionism makes things
Harder than they have to be
Creating disturbance
Patterns of anxiety
Hiding in the shadows
Of mentality

You must know the enemy before you can conquer him.

Alignment

Know how you want to feel

Why do we wait for things to get worse before we take action? Because we are dealing with our own dysfunction. It's really a tough job mastering yourself. We get started, experience conflict (minor or, major) become frustrated, stop and do nothing for weeks or months, but cannot stand the current state of our life.

Every day we have internal conversations regarding some minute detail of our existence. This is because we live in an environment that requires choosing between opposing realities. Go to work, stay home, eat, don't eat, drive, walk take the stairs etc. Everything is in contrast. Its seems unreasonably real-unreal. Real because projection is created by perception (which is unreasonable) and perception is based upon emotions and lies which create illusions—unreal. Confused?

The point is, most days we experience some level of fear and find ourselves backpedaling instead of forging ahead. We choose our waking experience daily. And when we experience heartache or disappointment, we cry and bellyache while waiting to be relieved or, rescued from the emotional pain of our own choosing.

Often, we choose what we know does not or, will not fit into our lives and become frustrated because we can't sustain what we've chosen. Even more we want it now or, have an all or nothing attitude in our approach and when it doesn't happen within our minimum time of investment we experience emotional turmoil.

There's no mayhem. Are you pursuing what you desire and feel connected to or, just doing something? You will not be able to sustain energy that is not really who you are. Your actions must be in alignment (agreement) with who you are or you will use your energy wrong and experience conflict. You can't do what's best for everyone because you end up compromising your own good feeling. And we all want the good feeling.

Once you experience and become comfortable in doing that which pleases you, you will find your power base. Sounds crazy, huh? What does this feel like? You will feel worthy, deserving and desirable—overall goodness. Know what I'm talking about now? It's really that simple. Being aligned feels good when you're connected and awful when you're not.

Many do not agree, because we do not want to be responsible for the condition of our lives. We push against the things we want. We go against the flow, travel upstream, but desire to be healed. You're going about things the wrong way. Our purpose is to experience joy and that will not occur until we learn to choose the path of least resistance.

Get aligned.

God Stuff

I'm sick of all the God stuff I hear!

Are you sick of all the God "stuff," you've been taught, learned, picked up, put down, forgotten and remembered? Well, are you? Are you on "I'll believe it when I see it street?" Have you allowed your experiences to shape your beliefs? It's a dogfight trying to stay positive, loving, hopeful and peaceful in a chaotic world because our human condition and experiences mold the perceptions we walk around in daily.

Stop. Step back. Breathe. Proceed.

If you don't feel like the word of God is working in your life, what's your stance? Are you studying, pursuing and applying it, or, are you just sitting back and expecting it to work upon your request? Faith is active. Strengthen your mind by reading the word of God. Give God a chance and stop deceiving and relying upon yourself. Rely upon and trust God. Bring your ego and issues to God. What do you have to lose?

Practice faith not self-sufficiency.

How do you see God?

Your connection or, lack thereof.

What is your concept or, image of the creator? How were you introduced to God? As Punisher...law maker...rule setter...judge and jury? In your thoughts, what is his character like? Is he concerned, available, unavailable, mean, parental, fearful, comforting, unfair, loving, unconcerned, or absent? Or, are you uncertain there is a God?

Whether you believe, or not, you show your faith through your concept of who He in your life. If you think of the creator as a punisher you expect to get punished; a ruler you expect rules; a forgiver you expect forgiveness; nonexistent you reject any reference and tell yourself there's nothing to fear. When you find yourself angry, disappointed or, rejecting God, usually it's the concept in your mind of who God is you're rejecting. You have to understand your concept (idea) of God, to know why you communicate with Him the way you do. Even the atheist refuses to realize he has a soul and communicates through rejection and a belief of accountability to oneself.

Yes, communication can become impaired but, not abolished. When you struggle with your perception of God

78

you are placing the condition of your thoughts on Him. Spirit is unalterable so there's no separation between the creator and his creations. Allow it to be what it is and feel like it feels for you. You are not self-made. Do not be fooled and think the energy of your spirit is neutral. The vibrational energy of the non-physical flows to and from all life. We cannot change the unchangeable.

Align yourself.

Where is God?

Power available to us.

Draw near to God and he will draw near to you. Do you believe that? If not, how can you expect to experience something in which you do not believe? If so, is the mind of your spirit obedient to God? Do you have an inner vigilance to submit to something higher than yourself? Or, do you reject the thought of such an entity?

Are you upset with God? Are you struggling with understanding how could He allow such painful things to happen? Do you blame God for your misfortunes? Do you believe you get what you expect? Does God owe you a certain type of life experience? Have you chosen the circumstances you've experienced yet, blame God for the outcome?   Have you been the unfortunate victim of a negative circumstance. You're not alone.

Until you make peace with God (if you believe) it will be difficult to live in peace and harmony with yourself or others. Although, it is people or, oneself causing hurt and injury, we tend to alter our relationship with God. Put forth an effort to keep your spirit aligned with your spiritual beliefs.

There has never been a promise ensuring avoidance of hardships or, challenges. Renew and deepen your faith when your relationship feels tested during troubling times. Seek the help of other friends of faith if you need. When you do, the spirit will lift you to a level of peace you can't achieve on your own. God's word is effective if it's in your heart. You have to pursue the word of God in order for it to work in your life. Seek and apply.

Put God first in your life.

Where Are You?

Do not choose functional disharmony.

Okay...here goes. Where is God? Where are you, is the real question.   How did you become disconnected?   What happened that caused you to turn away from God? God doesn't disconnect from us. We disconnect from Him

80

through our pain, anger, doubt, mistrust and distress. Know that, anything you accept apart from Him will deafen his voice in you. When we choose to be absent from Him, we believe He is absent from us. He is either everything or nothing; all in or all out. It's your struggle...you decide. His word tells us to stay connected no matter what we go through. But we get discouraged and frustrated; and often reject him. His hand is still on your life.

He never wanders away from us. He is not hiding from you. Nor, is he waiting to punish you. He is waiting for you to silence the chaos going on inside. "Be still, and know that I am God." (Psalm 46:10). This means cease striving; stop your fighting; return to me; be in awe and recognize; quiet your mind so, you can hear and receive the peace you seek. He waits for us to reconnect. There's no penalty for disconnecting or, turning away. Just more love and acceptance than you can fathom. Remember, there is no separation.

Desist.

Faith

Beyond belief.

Faith is trust and confidence that what we hope for will actually happen. Faith is not limiting like beliefs because faith says all things are possible. Faith says, believe even if you cannot perceive. It looks beyond circumstance, reasoning an understanding. There will be times your faith requires you to believe with evidence and believe without evidence. To experience living by faith you must choose and practice faith. Make time for God and your spiritual life.

Everyone has a measure of faith. As you apply faith, there will be times when it is strong and solid; confused and challenged; criticized and analyzed; and you realize the limits of logic. Spiritual mind like the physical body requires activity. Exercise and strengthen your spiritual mind by studying the scriptures, teachings and prayer. As you grow in spiritual knowledge and understanding your faith will strengthen. And, you will develop the courage to visualize, trust and act towards what you want to do, and where you want to go. Within, you have the thing you desire. Spiritual knowledge will bring you closer to God in all aspects of life, and guide you in action towards what you have reason to believe is true without physical evidence. Apply faith over and over and over again.

Respond to God and he will respond to you.

Is it hard to walk by faith?

Faith must be strengthened.

Practicing faith is hard because often we think and believe what the physical eyes can't see, does not exist. We want details and proof. The challenge about faith is there is no compromise. Nor, can it be rationalized or, explained logically to satisfy all questions. It's a decision to believe or, not.

Either you believe in spiritual sight and the idea of faith, based upon the principles or teachings of your understanding or, you do not. When you're doubled minded the purpose of faith is lost because it is not recognized. Make up your mind. You're either all in or, all out. Without faith, it is impossible to please God.

The other issue, is our propensity towards laziness and longing for ease. This causes most of us to work in weak faith. Strengthen your faith. Strengthen faith by studying the word of God (religious preference) relying upon it and training your will. Learn and practice applying faith. How? Choose faith (your firm standing) and show it by your actions. Instead of listening to the voice of doubt and uncertainty. Faith and actions work together. Yes, it is hard because the conscience is weak and we're accustomed to adhering to the reasoning mind—what you see and hear.

Looking at the big picture, our judgment is extremely faulty and we're not totally truthful. Often, we say we've turned a situation over to God but we haven't. Many of us have turned our salvation over to him but not our situation; not control of our lives. We say we are seeking his direction but, secretly we're not. We become impatient and try solve problems based upon our interpretation and want things done our way. We're absorbed by selfish interest—how things ought to be; and base truth on our feelings. This battleground is where fear attacks confidence and you experience defeat or, retreat.

Both knowledge and ignorance are known by the Creator. Being so, what you choose to believe is up to you. Faith requires consistency and because we are spiritual beings' faith reminds us there is spiritual sight. If you choose not to believe in a spiritual mind—something other than what you see—you will remain under the pinning of the trusted limitations of physical sight and logic; where judgment based upon the senses rule out possibly anything else. Perception is limited and can only take you so far. Don't make it harder than it is.

Recognize the sovereignty of God.

Where is your focus?

Obstacle or Opportunity.

So...do you believe there are unseen energies that may be seeking to sabotage your happiness? I ask because if you believe in other powers and principalities you will understand when I say falsehood and dishonesty are always seeking to conquer.

Being so, because we are spiritual beings living in physical bodies, residing in the physical world we can easily assume or, not realize what is going on. Because we function from the faculties of taste, touch, smell, hear and see, the physical world can distort what you think is true in the spiritual world. This is way bigger than human understanding, so it's not personal or just about you. However, you must guard your mind.

Is your faith strong yet, changes when a negative event occurs? If so, where is your focus? Is it on the problem or circumstance? Are your thoughts stemming from fear or, faith? In the morning, when you wake not feeling your best (spiritually), does this have anything to do with your faith?

Faith and feelings are not the same. Feelings based on thoughts and emotions—doubt and anxiety—can affect your faith, but they have nothing to do with faith itself. What's being revealed is your (mental) place of faith in regards to what is on your mind. This is what causes you to question if faith has changed. It has not. You have. Your faith isn't aligned with the word of God. Faith is a decision. You decide what to have faith in. Even the choice of having faith in nothing is a direction.

When things look gloomy, discouraging and seem against you, quiet your fears and control your thoughts. Examine your thoughts and choose to focus on what matters which are the promises of God. Don't allow situations to build up in your mind that causes confusion because this can impact your actions and behavior. If you need to discuss it, sit down and talk about it with someone you trust. We can all finish our race strong.

"Whatsoever is not from faith is
sin." (Romans 14:23).

Exhaustion

Burnout.

The busyness of living can cause burnout—physically, mentally, emotionally and spiritually. Because of demands on time and energy there will be times when you need to unplug—decompress. If you don't, stress will take its toll and you will experience exhaustion.

Our natural state of wellness is not weariness and fatigue. These signal overload. You have to keep a pulse on doing too much and trying too hard. You can't do zillion things at once. You were not designed to stay on or, plugged in. The body and mind need proper rest to restore and be productive. Know your limits and the areas of your life that need to be strengthened.

Perseverance requires strength in all areas to keep moving toward your goal. Grow and develop your spiritual life. You must have inspiration, faith and belief to pursue what you believe and manage the stressors of living. Stay in your lane; run your race; mind your business and work on yourself. Fight your fight not anyone else's. Don't waste energy participating in toxic situations. When you do, you lose focus about your own life and become side-tracked, distracted and tired.

Influence and persuasions are crafty. Pay attention to who you allow in your life and what you listen to. Who and what you are giving your energy to? What kind of vibration are you allowing yourself to be a part of? Be mindful of your inner conversation. The emotional baggage of past pain—hurt, (wounds), waiting, wandering, procrastination and doing too much causes exhaustion. You have to pay attention and know when you are repeating behaviors that do not lead you to where you want to be. This is what causes you not to experience joy. It's like trying to drive a car in the ocean or, buy shoes at the bank and wonder why you can't. Thus, you get mad at the creator and others after you experience exhaustion from choosing foolishness.

If you're exhausted, where are you investing your energy? What's on your mind that is consistently disturbing your peace? What thoughts are you turning over and over in your mind? Can you affect the outcome of the situation? If so, do your portion and release the rest. Release, meaning you have to learn how to let things be...be what they are going to be. This is hard but each soul has the responsibility of finding and creating peace and harmony while in the physical; to experience living more joy than pain. You must learn to stop allowing other people's misunderstanding of life, enter your joy.

Know and respect your limits.

Spiritual or Physical

Everything in the natural world fights against faith.

Thoughts are either focused on the spiritual or, physical world. But, not at the same time. This is not to say things cannot exist at the same time in the spiritual and the physical world. They can. Think about it.

When you enter a room, there are physical objects (chair, TV, bed etc.) and spiritual elements (air, atoms, space, sound). Both worlds are very real. Even though they both exist, they're opposed to each other and forever will be. They are not compatible because the desires are not the same. This is to guide you. To know which world, you're dominated by listen to your thoughts.

Stay focused.

Prayer

Why can't I sleep?

In prayer, don't be so occupied with whether or, how God is going to answer your prayer. When you're preoccupied, you experience anxiety, stress and emotional turmoil. Are you worrying, doubting?

Most times we keep praying and praying when we need to believe and believe. How do you behave? Where does your faith lie...over in want? How much time are you allotting God to fulfill your request? When do you get sick of waiting and give up hope?   Waiting and believing is tough, but it is our duty. What's the alternative?

Faith in Him, is also, our faith in ourselves. If your request return unanswered or, less than desired is that "proof" prayers are not answered? Is there unbelief at the bottom of your petition—your prayers to God? Careful, do not become your own counsel. If you struggle with unbelief, ask God to help your unbelief. You have to choose to back your faith with belief instead of unbelief. During this time, be of good courage. Be encouraged against oppositions and difficulties. Practice being faithful.

Even though you may feel unaccepting or, may not understand, God has brought you this far and is still with you. Walk by faith, seek his guidance. Do not be guided by your own counsel but, by his covenant with you. You cannot bargain with God. Do not stand in your own way blocking light with your logic, questions, doubt and unbelief.

God's thought are not our thoughts.

90

Prayer Is Not

Open your spiritual eyes.

Praying is not for the purpose of eliminating undesirable outcomes. It is for God's will to be done. God moves and speak according to his will not ours. It may take a while to accept this because we want to control outcomes and don't understand the will of God. No one does. Understanding is not required, our trust is. His love and joy is too deep for us to comprehend.

To our benefit, we have the word of God to trust in; not the word of our own mind. For we cannot count on or, trust in ourselves as with the Lord. Even though he may not do what you want, he never falters. His offerings to us never changed. Are you praying or, complaining to God? Do you believe God will not to allow a certain thing to happen in your life until he desires to do so? Do you believe he's holding or, keeping something from you? Are you shouting why and when, God? We all have these experiences. Our job is to "Trust in the Lord with all of our heart and lean not on your own understanding; in all your ways acknowledge him, and he will make your paths straight." (Proverbs 3: 5-6). Believe and trust in god, not your misconceptions. When we think wrong, we believe wrong. A divided mind reveals weak trust.

Learn to trust.

Prayer Is

Prayer is a process.

Prayer is communication between you and the Creator. Prayer should be focused. The time between your prayers and when you see things possibly manifest in your life, is a process. This process includes the unknown and unpredictable in the working out of God's grace in our lives.

Whatever you face keep moving forward in your trust. Prayer shows our dependence on God. We don't know the result. Do not misunderstand, when you disbelieve you side against. Do not equate prayer with getting, because it changes the value of your communication with the creator. Trust the process

Unbelief affects your faith.

Trust
You either trust or, you don't.

There's trust and doubt. When trust is an issue, the struggle reveals you're not completely trusting God nor, releasing the situation.

Most often we doubt that God or, person will fix a situation according to our hope. Yet, we must learn to trust the process. This process includes accepting two truths: 1) You do not know everything; 2) You will not understand everything. No one does. Trust requires vulnerability; there are many unsolved and unanswered questions.

For most, trust takes time to develop but, seconds to destroy. Unfortunately, there are people who prey on the goodness of others through the practice of deceit, lies and trickery for their advantage. They practice falseness in appearance and speech, make false promises, betray trust and use flattery to intentionally lead you down the wrong path. They have no good intent.

When things you don't understand happen, you must learn to rely upon your reservoir of inner strength to face difficult times or, you will experience panic and lack peace of mind. Remember evil operates to ruin your faith. "By good words, and fair speeches they deceive the hearts of the simple." (Roman 16:1).

Deceivers seek to slay your faith and deceive your heart. When this happens roll back to your roots—stay close to God. Where's your faith rooted? Depend on it regardless of how enticing or, dooming the situation may seem. Your conversations and actions must be in agreement, alignment with your belief. It doesn't matter if you don't understand how things will work out. "For just as the heavens are higher than the earth, so are my ways higher than your ways and my thoughts higher than your thoughts. (Isaiah 55:9).

Trusting this knowledge is how you walk by faith. Yet, this is where many of us falter. We become enticed by dishonest words or actions, fall prey, experience the pain of deceit and become angry at man and God for it all. And arrogantly think we're owed an explanation why our good intent wasn't protected.

Begin here. Were you caught up listening only to what you wanted to hear because you wanted something so badly? Did you fall for the promise of fast money, weight loss, instant fame, cure-all, good luck or, a longing fulfilled? Did it sound or, seem too good to be true?

Most times the ear cannot perceive the subtleties of deceitful motives. This is a rough terrain because I'm speaking about matters of the heart. And, you're probably saying, "I don't want to hear this!" Don't allow the emotional pain of being deceived fester or, turn to into rage. Deal with it. Guard your mind and heart. Do not pin your faith on another. If you believe in prayer, pray for wisdom and the ability to perceive and recognize this behavior. You will become more resilient. Continue to trust, love and hold yourself accountable. Begin again.

You can only control your actions.

Patience

Sigh...so not good at this.

God's waiting room. Living brings about a series of issues and conflicts. Either, you are in one now, just coming out of one or, heading into another. That's life. Stay focused, positive and prayerful because waiting can feel exhausting and discouraging.

Delay does not mean denial but it can be frustrating. Understand, if the thing you want hasn't happened, it doesn't mean it isn't going to happen. Are you expecting it to happen or, have you given up? Funny, we don't have a problem with waiting when things happen quickly or, go our way. But when we experience delay or, we get something other than we want, we question if the creator is looking out for us or, has our best interest. Weak-minded and easily swayed we are. Do not base God's character on your character. Use the time to prepare for that which you are waiting on.

When you rely on the world, worrying and fear increases. At all times, God is with you. Relying on God is a constant action. Every day it starts over. Reliance on faith develops patience. If it doesn't feel like your patience is growing it's because your thoughts continue to focus on the physical world—the senses. Don't say "If I'd known God was as slow as He is, I wouldn't have bothered Him." Just wait patiently. Stick it out. Have patience with God, for he is more than patient with you.

God isn't wasting your time.

THREE

I'm looking for something I cannot see...I know because I'm making room for me.

Doors are being opened for us all of the time...if you listen within.

Listen to advice and accept instruction, that you may gain wisdom in the future. -Proverbs 19:20

Three: Change Your Mindset (Make Room for You)

Woman Crisis

All of this stress and all of this mess
I'm living in a scattered consciousness
I've got, all of this stress and all of this mess
I'm living in a scattered consciousness

As the cancer eats away my breast
I must confess I never learned to see
about the woman in me

I learned to sacrifice and give advice
to always be nice and do everything twice
to compromise and wear a disguise
to gossip telling vicious lies
but never, ever celebrate and appreciate
the woman I see...
looking back at me
With failing health and seeking rest
An enlarged HEART lies within her chest

She says...
but what was I supposed to do?
the children needed me and my man did too
so, I... silenced my mentality
suppressed my sexuality
accepted infidelity
as so not to challenge masculinity
in a world that ignores the value of "she"

Three: Change Your Mindset (Make Room for You)

the societal rope around my neck
has kept me in check
see, I live in a place
where being feminine is, a disgrace
so... they cover my hair and cover my face
and put me in a space called gender

where I'm ruled by constant bouts
of surrender of self
so, you see, Eve is left
with only the social quality
of the rib that Adam gave to thee

my children are living in a generation
where foster care is the normal situation
sex trafficking and prostitution
often times seem my only solution

I got stiletto heels a pimp and a thong
exploiting my body using a pole and a song
I'm burning with desire and a need to confess
mastering lost libido, high blood and stress
working twice as hard, getting paid for less
I am a WOMAN IN CRISIS

I am "SHE"
who chooses to be male
I'm on my second marriage
because the first one was hell
I had my first baby before I was sixteen

Three: Change Your Mindset (Make Room for You)

and the names they called me
certainly, wasn't queen
I'm the wife, mother, sister and homemaker
the forgotten daughter locked incarceration

my sisters where are you in this mess
of gender bias consciousness?
we are living proof of MLK's dream
pledge with me to walk like a queen

I pledge
to think before I do
and rise each time I fall
because I am strong and beautiful
remember I am worth it all
treat others with respect
never give up on my dreams
ask for help and give it
because I am a
Queen

Freedom

The gift.

The gift of freewill is extraordinary, exciting and sometimes frightening. You have the freedom to choose whatever direction you want your life to go. The creator will allow you to travel the path determined by your thoughts.

Your will is as free as others, but it's collaborative. There's choice and agreement. Others can suggest and guide you. However, you choose to accept or, reject the guidance. Right or, wrong—the decision is yours. The challenge with freewill is taming the mind. The wild, unruly "will" must be trained to yield and submit to control and be of good service to the creator.

If you misuse your freedom you will suffer a loss of peace. All loss of freedom comes from wrong thinking and misunderstanding. Causing harm to yourself or, others is misuse of freewill. Pain and failure are the consequences of not cooperating with the laws created.

You must know the enemy to conquer him.

Acceptance

*Everyone has a moment where tomorrow
becomes real.*

Let's jump right in. You only get one body. Love and accept it. Big, small, short, tall, wide, thin, square, round, dark light, medium, cute or not-so cute—that's it. The order has been placed and shipped. Now it's your job to accept and love it. All systems are in working order by the designer and it's filled with spirit and covered by grace and mercy and you own it for a limited portion of time. It's time to accept, enjoy and live.

To experience freedom from your shadow of criticism and judgment you must learn to treat yourself in a respectful and appreciative manner. Otherwise you will sabotage opportunities that come your way and limit your potential for success. Why would you do this? Fear of success and failure. The power of this fear can create patterns of behavior that lead to futures you do not want. Confront your fear, accept yourself and make self-care a priority.

Acceptance is in direct proportion to what you can handle. Meaning, you may experience emotional pain and only be able to accept or, stomach so much truth about yourself. Why? As you become more conscious and aware of who you are, you begin to break away from the general collective mindset you've been operating in. This can be painful because you or, others may see your individuation as loss or separation. When it's really just growth and change. All, want acceptance for who we are, not the ridiculous idea someone may hold in their mind. Nothing to fear.

How do you talk to yourself? Are you kindhearted? Do you know yourself? Do you allow yourself to act foolishly? To know thyself, you must observe your behavior. This requires maturity, otherwise you will act willfully ignorant when you deal and cope with change and adversity. How so? Life is very different when you're in the sauce (the situation). You see how strong your inclination to shut down grows, how hyperrational and overly emotional you respond if things aren't going your way. You act negative and know it. Don't be divided against yourself only to feel embarrassed later. Know where your buttons are and don't push or allow them to be pushed.

Accept others. People are not going to respond the way you want or, think they should. Right or wrong, their response is based off of how they feel and what is perceived, just as you do. Accept this.

Learn to see things as they are and not how you'd like them. Mistaken certainty is usually based on your expectation of how things should be. Do not tell yourself lies about circumstances to avoid dealing with the truth. As long as you are in love with a lie you will not accept the truth about a situation.

Remember, everybody is learning, developing and growing. People can only give you the energy they live in, and vice versa. We bring our truest self (at that time) to the alter of interaction with the other soul. We give each other who we are but, we want something different. However, we're not always match for what we want. You attract what you are.

We're all a work in progress. Sometimes, what you want doesn't want you. You must know which lies you're in love with. Don't allow the energy of others to dictate how you pursue your happiness.

Become teachable. Everything isn't about you, actually nothing is. The universal lesson for all is growth. There are many things we assume are true and they're not. Don't be closed minded or, personalize all conflict. A disagreement is a disagreement. Do not impose your will upon others. Pride and competition causes conflict. Love thyself but don't be the only person you listen to. You're never the smartest person.

Love thyself.

Words

Life and death are in the power of the tongue.

Communication is the gift...let's get right into it. Words generate reactions so, watch what you say. They have meaning and evoke feelings in all creation. Even though animals can't speak they understand sound, pitch and tone. So, back to the basics—think before you speak. This is something all must practice over and over again. Don't say things you would not like said to you. Don't say things you can't take back. Once the words are released, that's it. We all forgive, but rarely forget. Speak kindly to all. When communicating with love ones, put forth extra effort to make sure loves nurtured. Build a solid foundation. And, when emotions get the best of you and you say the wrong thing, be mature and acknowledge your error. If necessary, apologize. Don't be a repeat offender using apology like a crutch.

Apology is to acknowledge a mistake, an error, not a soliloquy for intentional cruelty; a scapegoat for negative behavior. When you misuse apology, it becomes weak and ineffective. No apology erases intentional hurt. You can't control others or, their hurtful words, however you can remove yourself from their destructive impact upon your life. Avoid the language of argument. It creates distortion, deception and chaos in those listening.

You are full of what you've been saying. Every word you speak releases life or, death. Is the germ of defeat in your speech? Don't be deceived by slyness of words. Be mindful of your internal conversations. Do not go against your principles. Do not allow pain to cut off your ability to communicate. Be gentle with yourself. Tell your mind about God.

Words create thought. Feed your mind with positive words. Utilize the power within you to correct and create the changes you want to experience in your life. Take authority over your problems. You must encourage yourself. Always speak over yourself, problems and situation. Do not allow misery to gain power from your fear and pain. Speak to the mountains in your life; finances, health, relationships, emotions, etc. Stop waiting on God to do what he has given us the power to do, which is speak directly to the problem and create a plan of action to solve it. Do not release the enemy through negative talk.

Check your word diet. Is your vocabulary loaded with offensive, insensitive language? If so, you need a word detox. Find the source of your misery. What produces such poor communication? What is the root cause of your suffering? Are you angry, hurt, bitter, mean? Why attack others because of your unhappiness? You can only give others the energy you live in. Fix your life.

Guard the doors of your mouth.

Emotions

I am not my emotions.

We are emotional creatures having an emotional experience every day. However, you cannot let your emotions decide what is or, isn't possible for your life. Take responsibility. Learn to manage and control your emotions. They were given to us for a good purpose. Do not ignore or, pretend but manage them in a healthy way.

Monitor your thoughts to bring forth desirable conditions. Being ignorant of something does not change or, stop it from occurring. Emotionally, some things will be harder to move beyond than others but, don't be in the

107

mercy seat. Do not stay in sadness, madness or, any state of disharmony. Seek help if you need it.

The condition of your reality will continue to get your attention and use your emotions to do so. The challenge is not to let them dictate or, control your actions. Do not get caught up expecting a world according to your desires. Your perception of a situation can incite anger. Hurting yourself or, another never equalizes a situation. Choosing not to control your emotions give others power in your life. Create a balanced state of mind and make wise decisions.

What's at the end of negative feelings? Nothing good. Don't stay there. What you think about expands and grows. Fragmented thoughts impair judgment and good sense. This leads to foolish, regretful behavior—chaos and disharmony. And, you suffer from your own self-remorse. Do not let your conscience be captured by any of these: worry, indifference, shame, laziness, selfishness, pride, hatred, rage, vengeance, guilt, jealousy, procrastination, passivity, loneliness, deceitfulness...etc. Their root is fear and a sense of powerlessness.

Emotions do not determine what will be.

Self-Defeating

In-fighting.

Habit is everywhere. Society is ruled by good and bad habit. Just as there are habits that lead to success, there are habits leading to failure. Successful habits are what you should practice. Otherwise, prepare to experience disharmony within. Disharmony is a lack of agreement which doesn't correct itself—strife. Thus, you must investigate your own actions and behaviors to change your internal climate.

Negative habits serve the purpose of disconnecting you from "you." They distract you from truth. And ensure a pattern of staying on the wrong path of attempting to make the impossible work. Negative habits begin with the belief in a lie, practiced as truth which causes you to choose self-defeating behaviors. Self-defeating behaviors are nurtured when you act repeatedly from insecurities that create negative experiences. The result—hurry, mistake and injury—defeat.

Reality has a way of catching up with false thinking. After you collide with yourself a few thousand times you will come to the revelation that nothing else, nothing less than change has to occur. Listen to your thoughts to gain understanding of why you do that which is not good for you? How have you deceived yourself into practicing destructive behaviors over and over? What are you seeking to connect with? In order to change your direction, you must know what you are choosing. All actions and behaviors have consequences: positive, negative, intentional and unintentional. Negative habits such as: indecision, procrastination, self-pity, perfectionism, entitlement and resentment are sly. Don't become hostage to these mind-sets. Other habits: overeating, self-abuse, lying, depression etc... can interrupt your connection to the health principle causing you not to thrive.

Everything has not gone wrong. Change is possible. Turn around and stop fighting within. Make peace with yourself and decide to change. Strengthen your will, correct your thinking and stop mistreating yourself. Be accountable and seek help, if you need it. Do small things first. You will be glad you did.

Life is on our side.

Bondage

Self-imposed mental slavery.

Everyone, at some point in life, seeks relief from misery. Have courage. Whatever situation you got yourself into, you can get yourself out of. Careful not to condemn yourself by your past mistakes. Doing so, will lock your mentality and imprison the will. Do not choose this. It is self-imposed mental slavery.

Looking for someone to blame will not change where you are either. Despite how it may seem, you're not alone in your experience of hell, heartache or unintentional consequences. We've all made choices that led to suffering. You are where you are, and must take time and release what is of no benefit to you. Release requires action.

First, correct your victim mindset. Learning and applying is the quickest route to change. You need to learn something new. When you learn something different, you behave differently. Freedom from the bondage of pity requires different behavior. You must learn to think differently. Blaming society, people or, circumstances for poor decisions, inability to cope or, adjust to change will lead you to believe other things are in control of your life. This is not true.

Next, decide to change and follow through on your decision. Set the conditions which you must obey. Do not lose interest when it's time to take action. You owe you. Stop thinking and saying, "this is too hard," and quitting because you feel over-whelmed. Yes, it will be challenging.

But, problems do not dictate failure. You still have a choice, and the power to learn.

Work on your follow-through. Weak follow-through is a significant indicator of failure to progress. Self-pity and low-effort while hoping the situation will change will not lead to freedom. You must decide to work and hold yourself accountable. Or, continue feeling imprisoned by self-defeating behavior.

Be a first responder to your condition. Make yourself do the necessary things. Do what you can with what you have. Freedom from the misery of guilt, pity and shame requires discipline, sacrifice, commitment and prayer. Choose to release yourself or, continue to suffer the bond of iniquity living in quiet desperation. The choice is yours.

We aren't what we think we are.

Wilderness

Wilderness comes from choice.

Life, the Creator and love ones will accept the decisions and choices you make. However, when you make choices which fail or, do not turn out the way you want, resist the temptation to blame God or, others. Own, your stuff. You either did or, didn't do your best. These words are not to attack. They are to acknowledge truth. There is a difference in perceiving the truth and knowing it. You can't un-truth, truth.

The responsibility of freedom includes choice and agreement. And it should lead to freedom. If not, you know where you failed and what brought you to your wilderness experience. And, if you continue in the same way you will spend more time there. These are not penalties. These are natural laws; consequences. Like night, turning into day. Cause and effect: the disturbed inner world is the cause; the effect is the outer.

You may ask, "If God loves us so much, why doesn't he stop us from choosing self-defeating, hurtful behavior, we can't stop?" Because freewill and choice is our responsibility. God is not going to do what we can do for ourselves. You have the power to change every aspect of your life. If, He intervened, we would not understand the basic law of cause and effect. You must see and understand that you left your mind unguarded; and correction must begin where change is possible.

Therefore, unveil error, lies, dysfunction and disharmony. Otherwise, you'll persist in your nonsense. Know that conviction of behavior leads to correction.

Consequently, we're at our lowest when we decide to open our hearts, be humbled and respond to the source.

The kingdom is heaven is within you. Peace is our natural state of being and is found within, not outside of yourself. The wilderness happens when you accept false as truth. You will repeat your wilderness until you understand the powerful effect of lies, recognize the error you accepted as truth, and stop running from problems.

The good news is transformation happens in the wilderness and you can turn an upside-down world right-side up again. But it takes a team effort—you and God. Begin by correcting your mind and ask God what to do. You've been wandering long enough. Be a lamp unto your own feet.

"No weapon formed against you shall prosper." (Isaiah 54:17).

Stop List

Work on yourself.

- Stop wavering in the face of adversity.
- Stop judging yourself by your mistakes.
- Stop listening and agreeing with negativity.
- Stop disqualifying others; thinking you're better.
- Stop trying to make God's grace conditional.
- Stop saying I don't want to and I don't know.
- Stop shrinking when challenged.
- Stop procrastinating and being lazy.
- Stop complaining and whining.
- Stop making excuses; being indecisive.
- Stop tormenting yourself with doubt.
- Stop blaming others.
- Stop overanalyzing situations.
- Stop trying to become someone you're not.
- Stop personalizing situations.
- Stop talking and telling too much.
- Stop limiting and talking yourself out of things.
- Stop settling and choosing to fail.
- Stop quitting on yourself and others.
- Stop fretting, faking and pretending.
- Stop being double-minded and worrying.

- Stop self-promoting and giving yourself credit.
- Stop offering unwanted advice.
- Stop lying and manipulating.
- Stop creating unreasonable expectations.
- Stop being a slave to material possessions.
- Stop hating others success.
- Stop being afraid to try.
- Stop judging how others choose to live.
- Stop ignoring your issues.

How? Commit. When? Here and now.

Listen and Learn

Listen to learn.

You are exactly what you think you are, every day. What you feed your mind will impact the actions you take. What you listen to within the first twenty minutes of the day will influence how you approach the day.

When you think negatively, you believe negatively. Always seek to expand your awareness because your reality agrees with your logic. Listen to inner discussions because logic can cause you to work against yourself through excessive monitoring and questioning of outcomes. Often, it's your own ridiculous thinking that you must work your way around to avoid creating disharmony and hindering communication.

Listening actively is a skill and takes practice. When we choose not to listen actively and with empathy, we create gaps in communication. Often, we attempt to fill in the gaps with unwanted feedback when we should listen.

Explicit biases impact our ability to listen with empathy. Biases prevent us from examining new ideas. Most often, we sum up the person according to our perception or, scheme of things. Be reminded, this same process is happening when you speak. Be kind and allow others to speak, if it is of no harm. Practice tolerance. Respect other's perception. You may learn something.

Choose to listen. Not knowing how to listen handicaps your ability to learn, teach and understand. Practice listening to learn. When someone is sharing thoughts with you, they're not always seeking advice. Often, they just want to express or talk through what they are feeling.

Learn to offer advice or, feedback when requested. You are not the problem solver of others life situation. Think before you respond. Don't finish another's sentence. Understanding leads to change.

117

Learn to listen objectively. Don't get caught up in being right or, defending wrong to a fault. Communicate with others in the place of their awareness, not yours. Do not change the meaning, however, learn to alter the words if necessary. Don't insult by over-talking; speak to others on their level. Listen to learn. Become teachable. Too much talking leads to disaster.

Hush.

Esteem

Like to love yourself.

Esteem is formed by your perception of yourself. And it can hold you captive. Truthfully, the perception I had of myself held me hostage for years. I've watched this happen in the lives of others as well. It's not that they can't get passed others. They cannot get passed themselves without criticism or, negative comments. This self-talk occurs in the mirror, while driving or, at any other opportune moment.

The ego is childish. Its job is to distort the truth and create confusion between who you see and who you are. This is the function of vanity—excessive pride in oneself. There is danger in building your life upon what you look like, what you do or, what you have. Why? Because you will equate these things to self-value. Thinking, if you look a certain way, drive a certain car or, make a certain income increases your self-worth. The result is status envy; conceit—narcissism.

If you work solely for material enjoyment you will become dissatisfied and seek more of the same to relieve your suffering. Thus, polluting the mind and creating self-enslavement to material things and qualities.

Recognize when you're being corrupted by your ego. Do not seek praise from others based upon superficial values. If so, your efforts will become dependent on receiving praise and approval, and comparison and competition will become your goal. And you will base your success off of false standards. This game is unwinnable.

It's not wrong to enjoy material things. You are going to want material things because you are in a physical body, but you must close the gap between who you are and who your life has caused you to become. There is a difference. Recognize your own true worth.

How you feel (think) about yourself is who you present to the world every day. Is that really who you are? Unchecked poor or low esteem will continue to destroy your life as you age. Work to correct any distortions.

Personal self-acceptance and self-love is positive self-esteem. This is not egotistical. Don't be seduced by value judgment or, images. You are unique. However, do not think too high or, low of yourself. Do not walk around in self-praise. Or, you'll begin and end with yourself.

Create balance. You can never be better than your self-esteem. When you look at yourself, does the 12, 16, 20-year-old person you were, agree with the person you see in the mirror today? Love yourself.

"As a man thinketh in his heart, so is he." Proverbs 23:7

Health

Be well.

Health is a principal of the living substance. Health is the natural function of all the systems—mental, physical, emotional and spiritual—performing voluntarily, as perfectly designed. Within the design of the system, is the ability to heal itself. Health has all the life we will ever live. Therefore, health is a most precious gift.

Health affects all activity. Be a good steward over your health. The performance and function of each system, when in activity, cannot meet its goals without good health. If the health principle does not function properly success in other areas of life will be impaired—mental, social and physical. We have been given a body and are responsible to take care of its systems to make sure they perform optimally. This isn't a "should." This is a must. If you choose not to, you will experience the consequences of poor health. Perfect health and peace are yours for the asking. Give attention to the mental, physical, emotional and spiritual aspects of your being.

Being able to feel love towards yourself is key to mental health. Many of us have never been taught self-love. We're taught self-denial, sacrifice and to put others first. This is not correct. You must be able to love yourself so, that you can love others. Feeling sorry for yourself or, depressed is not a healthy state of well-being. It takes time to learn and know how to heal your inner sickness. You must find your mental traps and dismantle and disempower them. The power is through self-love and respect. You must learn to treat yourself like you treat your best friend, because that's exactly who you are. If you are a hazard to yourself, seek help.

Stress is an enemy. You must get rid of it; and you can. If you allow it to overtake any system, it will ruin your life principle. Overcome anxiety, worry and fear by controlling what you focus on. Recognize the voice in the shadows of your mind (critic, worrier, victim, saboteur). This entity will always strike with negative conversation.

You only get one body; listen to it and pay attention to the promptings and signals it gives you. Trust and do not ignore your intuition. Do not allow fear of the unknown, convince you not to act or manage your health principle.

Raise your awareness to make healthier decisions. Misuse and abuse of the body systems lead to irreversible consequences. Negative behaviors will produce negative outcomes. You pay now and later. Your health principle is designed to give back to you exactly what you give it. So, choose wisely.

If you're struggling with illness or, physical limitations, your health is still invaluable. Draw near to God and believe in your power and healing. Perfect health and peace is available. The condition requires your faith, belief and action. Something has to arouse your principle of health to become active to generate healing from within. You could be ill and on your way to wellness but, because you don't see evidence you convince yourself that healing is not occurring.

Do you believe more in sickness than wellness? What governs your thoughts? What remedy has your faith? Is it prayer, medicine, science, meditation, homeopathy, food or, mental affirmations? What needs manipulating in your thinking (beliefs) to arouse your principle of health?

You cannot have faith in health and think like a sick person. Take the time to improve your attitude towards healthy living. Rest, relax and restore. Pay attention and follow the good feelings that lead to your healing.

Well-being is well worth being.

Help

Serving others.

When you help others, you help yourself. We're all deficient in some area of our life. Our troubles may be different but, the pain of living is similar and behind the need for help is the longing for a better life situation.

Help comes in many forms: words, kindness, support, money, material, time, substance. Believe it or not, God is in control and the world is not doomed. There's only one power, presence and plan. Give expression to him by what he does through you. God does not need anything from us.

Help is not keeping a record of the things you've done for another. This is not help. This is self-promotion. Mistakenly, you believe you deserve credit for your actions.

If this is your mindset, correct it. We are no greater than each other. Don't become small-minded through judgment of those that may need more help than you. Everyone experiences difficulties and you will receive your portion. You may possess more material and resources; but you have no greater grace or, mercy than your fellow man. You are not a god amongst inferior beings. See and meet others as equals.

Help yourself and seek help if you need it. There's no shame. If there is, take the steps to deal with it. You have the responsibility of taking care of the life you've been given. Not, for others to take care of it for you. If you are receiving help, watch out for the attitude of entitlement. No one owes you anything. That doesn't mean others do not care. It means you have a responsibility and the capacity to get better and do better. Your life must matter to you in order to change it. Learn to be grateful, appreciative and accepting of the help the creator has sent to assist and share goodness with you. Pay it forward by sharing it with others.

We need each other. When I recognize the interest of the "whole" of something, I can then see how my part affects it. I must see and know this. Otherwise, I will behave as though what I do only affects me singularly, not realizing how the disturbance of self-centered behavior affects all of us because we are from One source and every soul matters. Help others. Move fearlessly and follow the leading of your spirit.

Begin helping at home. Check your manner and attitude within your family. Do not become a slave to others by waiting on them too much. This creates co-dependency and handicaps the individual. Everyone has their own journey so, do not over compensate for those that are unwilling to help themselves.

Worry is not how you help yourself or, others. Therefore, be mindful of the actions you take that are generated by fear. Providing help is different than becoming your brother's keeper. Meaning, you cannot be everything to everyone. Only the Creator can do that. He is a flowing source to all of his creation. You must learn how to help and also how to allow. Demonstrate your faith by doing your part and trusting God to take care of that which only God can take care of. You must learn to let things be.

God has our back.

Laugh

At yourself!

Laugh at yourself. Learn to see the humor in situations. Share your struggles with someone who understands and will help you see the humor in it. There's relief in laughter.

Don't take life too serious. Don't create stress about things which you have no role or, control over. Value communication, but don't over concerned yourself with what others will think. Reality changes quickly when you tune into the negative vibration and energy of others. And you can exhaust yourself through worry and frustration. Don't make life feel like it's too painful to enjoy. This is not our purpose. Joy is.

We all contribute enough time and attention to things that don't really matter. Don't get corrupted by life. Don't waste time trying to understand or, interpret the behaviors or, choices of others. Even though you love them, remember they're on their journey as well.

Put energy into pursuing what you want; and enjoy the taste of it while you can. Doing so, will help you transcend adversity and keep you from wearing a cloak of frustration when things don't turn out the way you hoped.

Learn to celebrate and appreciate the lessons life gives you. Do things for yourself. Care about you. Follow the good feelings often and live life on your terms. Breathe, everything is fine.

Love.

Dream

Believe. Create. Achieve.

Keep your dream alive. Make it clear. It is the vision you will build your life upon. Your vision is the promise of what you will become if you pursue it. You must have a hunger for what you want if you intend on accomplishing it. What are you passionate about? What are your motivations?

Wandering around is no fun. Begin today to act on your passion and desires. They will never leave you. You know what you're supposed to do because it feels right when you do it and it brings you joy. Become who you are. You are great by design, let it show it in your actions.

Dreams do not have to be grand or, over the top. Your dream is whatever brings joy to your life—going to school, buying a home, starting a family, changing careers, beginning or, ending a relationship, learning a language or,

127

instrument, serving others, retiring, traveling, buying a car, starting a business, investing or etc.

Have faith in your ability and fulfill your goals. Don't doubt yourself. Trust your intuition, believe what it tells you and obey your soul. It is your decision to live or, bury your dreams. Remain humble and grateful. You must believe what you want for yourself and your family, is possible to achieve it. How do you want to live?

Dream big.

Prepare

Changes the direction of your life.

Preparation is work. Don't expect or, waste time wanting things to be easy. You must work for what you want and prepare to take advantage of opportunity when it shows up. Be committed to putting in the work and beyond to change the direction of your life. Wake up earlier, go to bed later, attend seminars, pray, network, commit, avoid social media—this is your time to prepare—get it done. Be willing to devote hours to your craft to prepare for the opportunities you seek. Only you know what you have to offer people.

Truthfully, we all have something to give to creation and change is possible no matter where you are. Take a chance and believe in yourself. Move through the things that hold you back. If you don't like your life rewrite the script. The choice is yours to live life the way you desire. Only you know who you are.

Setbacks

Do not be afraid to fail. You only get better by perfecting your craft. When preparing, at some point you will experience setbacks or, failure. Failure is not final. I've learned that "FAIL" stands for First Attempt in Learning.

Failing is necessary so we can grow, become, change, try, accept, account and act again. Loss, defeat and failure exposes you to you. Failure leads to victory. It's the most real feedback you're going to get. It is the raw truth of where you need to challenge and improve, if you expect a better outcome. It exposes the weak areas you need to strengthen, let go of or, redefine. And, it reveals a true picture of your discipline and commitment. It's the ultimate face-off.

Put in the work.

Action

Decide. Commit. Act. Succeed. Repeat.

We're blessed. Every day we have life, time, gifts, grace, promises and opportunity on our side. Success is yours, if you're interested. Take action toward your goals and dreams to create a more enjoyable life. You'll always get out what you put in. Rise up to your potential. What's the alternative? Staying stuck? Not taking action is an action. You choose by default. Give yourself permission to do and have what you want. Tell yourself the truth. Feel uncomfortable and uncertain and take the action you need.

Taking action leads to growth. Wake up. Commit. Let go of your procrastination. Do the work required. Expect challenges. This is what you want. Do not settle for anything less than what you deserve. Go after what makes you happy. Get real with yourself. See more solutions than problems. Your circumstances will change when you change your actions. Take action that lead to the outcome you desire. Raise your level.

Decide. Commit. Act. Succeed. Repeat

Discipline

Requires sacrifice.

Your life is not going to improve or change on its own. You must take action. Once you accept and agree with this you will be able to see your patterns and understand what prevents you from achieving your desires.

To break patterns and do things differently you must make yourself do the things you don't want to do. This is discipline. Train your mind and body to follow the commands you give it. Stop waiting to feel like doing a certain thing. You're probably never going to feel like it because you're underdeveloped and weak in certain areas. And, perform at lower levels than required for the results you seek. The only way to get things done is to get things done. Discipline requires you to step outside of your comfort zone and think higher healthier thoughts. Replace old habits, create new ones and press forward. Get rid of the unrealistic expectation of instant gratification, comfort and ease.

Discipline is where you get things done. Discipline requires consistent behavior. Keep promises to yourself. Don't allow weak thoughts of self-pity rule your confidence. Discipline reveals the character behind your personality. It

131

shows how committed you are to your goals. Practice doing things that are right for you whether you feel like it or, not. Stick to, complete and finish something. Discipline is the key to changing life, and will lead to success.

Discipline leads to freedom.

Willpower

Get to the next level.

What is willpower? It is the ability to master your impulses. It is the key to staying in the game and on top of the game. Willpower leads to the next level; where you begin living out your dreams. You must train your will if you want to reach your greatest potential because it is critical to the level of success you experience.

Willpower is the heart of happiness. And, you must develop it. To train the will, you must consistently work to break and end patterns of negative energy and unwillingness. In order to break patterns and resist negative impulses, you must control your urges. This is not easy.

The negative habits you have must be replaced. Stay in control of impulses by performing right actions. Right actions build willpower and require commitment.

And, demand that you stop doing what you know does not work or, result in a negative outcome such as: excessive snacking, overeating, over-spending, sleeping in or, staying in bed, lying, being late, abusing alcohol or, other substances, playing video games, addictions: social media, porn, gambling, strip clubs, smoking, sweets, TV, negative friends or, any other energy draining low-level zombie-like, time-wasting activity.

The will is like any other muscle. If you don't use, train and develop (brainpower) it, it will atrophy just like your muscles when you don't exercise. Thus, you feel weak and wallow and continue to give up before you even try. A trained "will" fuels discipline and creates follow through. Sure, some days you will have to push yourself. But there's satisfaction in knowing you put forth your best effort and formed new habits.

Willpower and discipline determines how far you will go. You owe it to yourself to do the best you can to improve your life and results don't lie. Strongly developed willpower prepares you for the opportunities you seek. Besides, no one else is going to do it for you.

Grow your will. Increase your power.

133

Opportunity

Move with the flow

Be open and prepared to receive what is already yours. The creator responds to the vibration you give off and waits for your reception. See what's in your mind and continue to move in the direction of you, regardless of what you see. Do not look at things that do not match your desires. Look for the experience you're searching for. You will draw it unto yourself. But, you must be prepared to receive it.

Practice what you desire to become. Focus your dominant thoughts on what you want to experience. Do not lose heart, for you cannot become anything less than what you've become in your mind unless you choose to become less. Express and experience in the physical what you desire from within. The key, is you must be committed and work towards it. Move with, not against the flow.

Do the thing you need to do to experience the thing you want to experience. Draw in the vibrations you desire to change your reality. You have everything you need and will receive what you are not aware of. Decide how you want to feel about something and then look upon the situation. Instead of looking and allowing your emotions to tell you how you should feel about that which you see.

Seek more and you will experience more. Keep moving in the direction of the opportunity you seek. Don't allow your actions to decrease due to things you can't control.

When you struggle, you're pulling back against what you've asked your "true" self to hold for you. You're fighting with your inner being which is only trying to help you become who you are. Often, we attempt to go in a direction different than where we should be going. This was my wrong habit. I had to stop trying to do things my way and stop pulling (going against the flow).

Opportunity is not something you can always see because it doesn't manifest exactly as you've imagined. However, when you experience it, it fuels and satisfies your desire and you know it. You'll feel overwhelming but exact. Although it may seem like you're going backward, you are not. So, don't overthink actions. Keep moving forward toward your desires. Trust that you have enough of what you need. You just have to use it. Lift yourself higher, brighter, bigger and you will see everything is exactly how it's supposed to be. You will receive all you need and more.

If you disagree, have you unknowingly practiced feeling unworthy and undeserving of that which you desire? What has been your experience? Maybe your focus is in the past. Do you doubt your self-worth or judge yourself harshly? Are you un-deserving of a healthy relationship, job, family, home, travel, finance, health etc.? Is this your mindset? If so, you will continue to feel out of sync, doubtful and uninspired.

Opportunity awaits you.

Hope

You are not forgotten.

Even when in doubt, there is a purpose for your life, and forever will be. Yes, there will be seasons of doubt and pain, but never lose hope that all is alright. The creator is on our side and promise to never to leave or, forsake us. If, you believe. No doubt, it's hard to move forward when you don't understand what is happening in your life. But, remember we're taking steps to create a quality life. Hope and long waiting are often part of the process.

When suffering, or going through pain, life is not against you. Growth happens through pain. Continue to believe in yourself and show faith by stepping into the unknown—trusting all is well. The best has not happened.

Don't waste time living a life that doesn't make sense to you. Daily, continue to work diligently and harmoniously because you're guided and supported even though you cannot physically see what you hope for. Society and your inner critic will tell you you're unworthy, forgotten and, to give up. Don't believe or, submit to this ill-thinking. At times, you may not feel it, but the creator's hand is on your life because we are directly connected to the divine source. Trust your intuition and the promptings you receive within. Listen and clear your mind of distorted beliefs and patterns of behavior that produce negative outcomes.

Even after I'd done everything, I still experienced negative compensation and hopelessness. Something was still missing. I was not who I wanted to be. I didn't have what I desired. I was busy doing what I thought I needed to do. I didn't know how to do what I loved because I didn't believe what I wanted, wanted me. And, I received exactly what I'd expected—unfulfillment. True, I accomplished lots of things but, I had not taken the steps or, put forth the effort to do what made me feel good and satisfied most of the time. By focusing on other things, I created a life of contentment and was silencing the voice of my potential, which was the screaming to be released.

Reality is a different frequency than your true desires. Get in alignment with the energy of your desires so, you can manifest them into being—create a new reality.

The one you want. If your hope has taken a beating, remember the biggest enemy, you have to deal with is yourself. You can have all you are capable of. Don't give up. You can start again. There's no straight path to success, but there's always hope. The answers lie within.

Be encouraged.

Today

There is NO struggle

What matters is now. Not your past, not tomorrow, but now. Be inspired! Today is new. Today, let's not doubt or, question the creator's love or protection for us. Let nothing disturb your peace. Look upon others as you desire to be looked upon. Choose to give thanks and express love. Rise above and join me in the awareness that we are from the One source. Love those you love, those that love you and those that need love. If you can't accept this thought today, I trust you will receive it when you are ready. Figure it out as you go and grow. We're all on the same journey. Become what you believe you can become. Live life as you wish.

You are here.

Now What?

By now, if you've finished My Way and seriously want to change your life, you've began doing the things you don't want to do. That's the bottom line. You have to practice doing the things that will lead to the positive outcomes you want. This needs to happen whether you feel like it or not. More than likely, you're never going to feel like changing the way you think about the way you think. You just have to get started. **That's the biggest step.** Now what? Start now. Take action.

If you've read this book and only thought of who this is applicable to, then you haven't received the message intended. I ask that you read it again. Why? Because personal development is personal. You have to apply what you've learned to your life and your fear.

The universe gives us what we desire, but, it can only give us what we allow. The problem is we ask for something and don't really believe we can have it. And when it doesn't happen we get discouraged. It's no secret, you receive what you believe.

We cannot have or, receive what we desire until we come into alignment with the thing we desire. That means, you have to know what you want, why you want it and focus on the experience of having it. You have to align your actions, behaviors and thinking with the desired experience and work to create it. In time, it will come to fruition. This book is proof for me, and you're no different than I. Take the time to listen. Go beyond your initial understanding of the *lessons within and apply as needed. They will change your life.*

Take the time to know yourself. Knowing takes time and requires study and meditation. You must search the mind to know why and what needs to be changed before you can apply new information to correct wrong thinking and old habits. Read and share this book, as often as needed. As you grow in your awareness you will be inspired and take action to create the life you desire and deserve...because you're worth it. I welcome all feedback.

Please visit iCreativProverti.com or, email me at db@iCreativProperti.com.

Thank you

Made in the USA
Middletown, DE
09 September 2024

60063788R00092